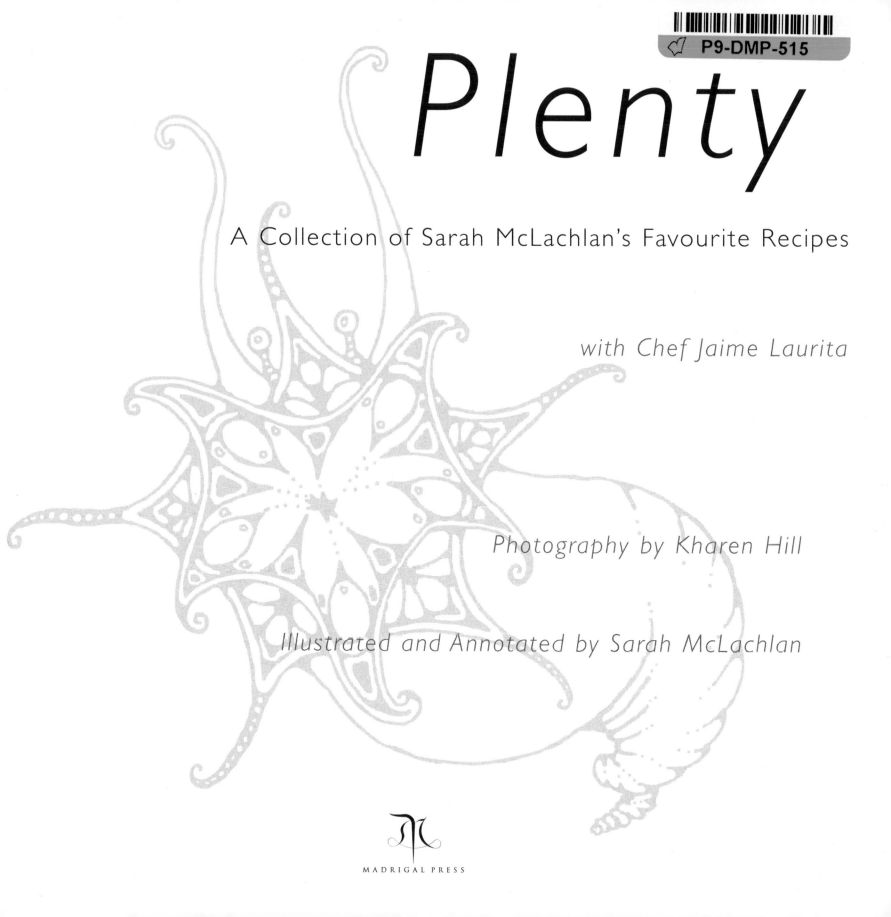

Plenty

A Collection of Sarah McLachlan's Favourite Recipes

with Chef Jaime Laurita

Photography by Kharen Hill

Illustrated and Annotated by Sarah McLachlan

MADRIGAL PRESS

Foreword

Besides music, good food has always been one of my passions. When I was a child, my mom always made sure that we ate delicious, wholesome food. She always baked her own bread, and my brothers and I always had an endless supply of delicious cookies and pies baked with love and care.

When I started touring, it became a real challenge to have healthy, consistent meals. We'd tour for months on end, sleeping on the bus, and for the most part we ate really dull, greasy food. Not being able to have the comfort of good food could really affect morale. Jaime came on board in 1997 as the official caterer for the band and crew. The change was amazing. Jaime is as dedicated to his craft as everyone I work with, and soon the mumbles and grumbles of "not veggie lasagna again" were replaced by "I can't believe he hasn't cooked the same thing twice!" We were all so happy to have someone with Jaime's care and dedication on board.

This cookbook came about for many reasons. I really wanted to be able to share the experience of Jaime's food with my friends. I also think that Jaime has a lot to offer to the cooking world—his tour cooking is at par with some of the best restaurants I've eaten in, and he always manages to make the food taste and look fantastic, even in the middle of nowhere. But the biggest reason is now I won't have to bug Jaime constantly for his recipes!

These recipes, tested and photographed predominantly in my home, cross a number of different cultures and food styles, from Thai to Indian, Mediterranean, Italian and Japanese. Also included are some of my own favourite recipes, and even some recipes handed down to me by my mom. Most are quite simple to prepare, but we threw in a few more difficult ones for the folks who like the challenge. I hope you enjoy these recipes as much as I do...

Bon Appetit!

Sarah McLachlan

Meet our chef, Jaime Laurita,
standing in front of what we call *home*
for most of the year.

It's such *a luxury*
to have *a real chef* on tour with us,
because his *great food* makes the road
feel a little bit more like home.

vii

Okra

Gooseberry

Lemon Grass

Chanterelle

Woodear

Oyster

Cilantro

Thai Basil

Galangal

Ginger

Leek

Ancho

Thai (red hot)

Anaheim

Habañero

Ancho-Pablano

Peppers

Portobello Mushrooms

Shallots

Fennel

Savoy Cabbage

Yellow Bell Pepper

Thai Eggplant

Japanese Eggplant

Butternut Squash

Acorn Squash

Appetizers

When I first moved to Vancouver eleven years ago I had never even seen an avocado, let alone tasted one. They just didn't have them in Halifax, Nova Scotia, when I was growing up. Now I can't believe I ever lived without them!

Although guacamole is usually served as a dip, it can be paired with anything, from fajitas to burgers to salad. When preparing this dish be sure to wear gloves when removing the seeds from the jalapeños. The oils from the pepper can really irritate your hands.

Guacamole
serves 4–6

- 4 very ripe avocados
- 1 small jalapeño pepper
- 1 medium tomato, seeded and chopped
- 3 tablespoons chopped white onion
- 3 tablespoons chopped red onion
- Juice of 1 lime
- 2 tablespoons chopped cilantro
- 2 cloves garlic, chopped
- ½ teaspoon chili powder
- Salt & pepper to taste

Peel and pit the avocados and chop into chunks. Remove seeds and membrane from jalapeño and discard. Mince. Mix remaining ingredients together with the avocado and minced pepper.

Tip: Save the avocado pits and put them in the guacamole, especially if you have to refrigerate it for a few hours before serving. The pits will keep it a fresh green colour.

We served the guacamole in a martini glass and garnished it with thinly-sliced fried potatoes.

Jaime has a great *passion for food.*
His attention to detail, from meal planning to presentation,
made a big impression on me.
Trying to decide *what recipes* should go
in the book was no easy task
because they're all *so good!*

Tequila Salsa
makes 1 party bowl

- 1 pablano pepper
- 2 jalapeño peppers, diced small
- 1 large white onion, diced
- 1 large red onion, diced
- 2 green onions, sliced
- 10 cloves garlic, chopped
- 1 red pepper, diced
- 1 yellow pepper, diced
- 1 green pepper, diced
- 10 red vine-ripened tomatoes, diced
- 4 yellow tomatoes, diced (if available, otherwise use red tomatoes)
- 2 large cucumbers, peeled, seeded, and diced
- 1 bunch fresh cilantro, chopped
- ½ cup canola oil
- ⅔ cup V8 juice
- ¼ cup tequila (optional)
- Juice of 2 limes
- Tabasco sauce to taste
- Salt & pepper to taste

Place pablano pepper on a baking sheet and broil until almost completely blackened, turning as necessary. Remove from oven, place in a bowl and cover. When cool, peel and discard the skin and seeds. Dice.

Wearing gloves, prepare jalapeño peppers by removing seeds and membrane and discarding. This can be done under running water. Dice. Remove gloves and wash your hands, being careful not to touch your eyes.

In a large bowl, toss all ingredients together. That's it!

This easy-to-prepare dish is basically toast points with delicious toppings. There are literally hundreds of things you can put on top of toasted, crusty bread. Try hummus, olive tapenade (olive purée), baba ghanouj (eggplant spread) or cheese spread. This is the classic Italian bruschetta, which is very simply topped with tomato salad—a great dish to take to a party.

Bruschetta

serves 6

Topping
- 2–4 large ripe tomatoes
  (vine-ripened are preferred)
  4 fresh basil leaves, chopped
- 1 tablespoon capers
- 3 tablespoons chopped onion
- 3 cloves fresh garlic, chopped
- 4 tablespoons olive oil
- Splash of balsamic vinegar (optional)
- Salt & pepper to taste

Toast Points
  1 loaf crusty Italian bread
- 1 or 2 cloves whole garlic, peeled

Cut tomatoes in half and remove seeds and pulp. Cut into bite size pieces. Add basil, capers, onion, garlic, olive oil, balsamic vinegar, salt and pepper and chill until ready to serve.

Slice the bread and toast it lightly. When cooled, gently rub with garlic, being careful not to crush the bread. To serve, simply spoon the tomato mixture on top of the toast points. If you're going to take these to a party, assemble them when you arrive. It only takes seconds and the toast points will stay crisp longer.

Hummus is an easy dip to make for large groups of people. Start out with the basic recipe and adjust the flavours to taste, adding anything from fresh chopped dill to hot chili powder. Try serving it on your favourite sandwich, as an accompaniment to fajitas, or thinned out as a salad dressing.

Hummus

serves 6

- *3 cups canned garbanzo beans,*
  drained and rinsed
- *2 tablespoons tahini*
- *3 tablespoons chopped garlic*
- *3 tablespoons lemon or lime juice*
- *Salt & pepper to taste*
- *1/4 cup olive oil*

Blend ingredients together in a food processor. If you don't have one, use a hand blender. Add olive oil and thin to desired consistency. For a low-fat version, use warm water or vegetable stock instead of olive oil. Chill and serve.

For an interesting variation add:
- *1/4 teaspoon toasted mustard seeds*
- *1/4 teaspoon toasted cumin seeds*
- *1 tablespoon almond or walnut oil*
- *1 tablespoon sesame oil*
- *2 tablespoons chopped fresh ginger*
- *1 1/2 tablespoons chopped cilantro*
- *3 tablespoons chopped mint*
- *1/4 teaspoon garam masala*

Toast mustard and cumin seeds over medium heat for about a minute in a dry frying pan. Add all ingredients to the basic hummus. Chill and serve.

This refreshing dish can be served as a dip or as a light summer soup.

Tzatziki

serves 6

- *4 cups plain yogurt*
- *1–2 garlic cloves, chopped*
- *3 tablespoons chopped mint*
- *8 small cucumbers, peeled, seeded*
  and diced
- *Salt to taste*

In a mixing bowl, beat yogurt until smooth. Add garlic and mint. Stir. Add cucumbers. Let marinate a few hours in the fridge before serving.

This Middle Eastern eggplant dip is great when paired with pitas, chips or even spread on a grilled vegetable sandwich.

Baba Ghanouj
serves 4

- *1 medium eggplant*
- *¼ cup tahini*
- *¼ cup lemon juice*
- *1 garlic clove, chopped*
- *1 teaspoon olive oil*
- *1 teaspoon chopped parsley*
- *Dash of Tabasco*
- *Salt to taste*

Preheat oven to 350°F

Cut eggplant in half. Place flat-side down on an oiled baking sheet and bake until the insides are cooked and very soft, about 15–20 minutes. Cool. Remove the insides with a spoon.

Puree the eggplant, tahini, lemon juice, garlic and olive oil together. Stir in parsley. Add Tabasco and salt to taste.

Spinach Salad with Honey-Orange Dressing
serves 4

- *1 bunch spinach, cleaned*
- *1 large carrot, grated*
- *1 Granny Smith apple, peeled, cored and chopped*
- *1 orange, peeled and sectioned*
- *2 tablespoons black raisins*
- *1 tablespoon golden raisins*

Toss all of the above ingredients together in a bowl.

Dressing

- *¼ cup canola oil*
- *3 tablespoons orange juice*
- *1 tablespoon honey*
- *1 teaspoon ginger, powdered*
- *½ teaspoon minced garlic*
- *Pinch of cinnamon*
- *Salt & pepper to taste*

Mix all the dressing ingredients together. Toss the spinach and dressing together right before serving.

This classic salad is best prepared with the freshest ingredients possible. A high quality olive oil rounds out its naturally delicious flavours. Fresh buffalo mozzarella can be used to make this dish extra special. It can be expensive and difficult to find, so bocconcini, a soft unripened mozzarella, is an excellent alternative.

Caprese Salad with Roasted Zucchini

serves 4

- 2 large zucchini, sliced
- Salt and pepper
- 1 tablespoon freshly chopped rosemary
- Olive oil
- Balsamic vinegar
- 4 large vine-ripened tomatoes
- ¾ lb bocconcini or mozzarella cheese
- 6 large basil leaves, cut into strips

Preheat oven to 350°F

Place zucchini in a bowl with salt, pepper, chopped rosemary and just enough olive oil to coat. Place on a baking sheet and bake 15 minutes or until lightly browned. Remove from the oven and cool. Sprinkle with balsamic vinegar.

Slice the tomato and mozzarella into ¼ inch slices and interlayer with the zucchini. Drizzle with olive oil and garnish with basil.

For an interesting variation, try serving Caprese Salad with whole cherry tomatoes.

We sometimes *spend months* at a time away from home *travelling around* like nomads. There's often little consistency, so great tasting, *healthy food* offers a lot of comfort in an always changing environment.

The mess tent

Caesar Salad

serves 4

- *2 egg yolks*
- *1/3 cup olive oil*
- *1 tablespoon red wine vinegar*
- *Juice of 1/2 lemon*
- *1 tablespoon Worcestershire sauce*
- *1/2 teaspoon dried mustard*
- *2–4 garlic cloves*
- *3 anchovies or 2 teaspoons anchovy paste*
- *Salt and pepper to taste*
- *1 head romaine lettuce*
- *1 cup grated parmesan cheese*

Beat egg yolks with a wire whisk. Slowly drizzle in olive oil, continuing to whisk. Stir in red wine vinegar, lemon juice, Worcestershire sauce and dried mustard. Chop the garlic and mash it together with the anchovies until a paste forms. Stir into the egg mixture. Add salt and pepper to taste and set aside.

Carefully wash and dry the lettuce. With clean, cool hands rip the lettuce into bite size pieces. Toss with the dressing and sprinkle with grated parmesan. For a spectacular display, place whole lettuce leaves on each plate and drizzle the dressing over top. Top with freshly grated parmesan.

This easy recipe makes a nice summer dish. Its sweet and savory flavours combine to make an exciting and adventurous taste sensation.

Fennel-Calamari Salad

serves 6-8

- 6 small calamari (fresh or frozen)
  cleaned and cut into rings
- 2 bulbs fennel, cored and thinly sliced
- 5 navel oranges, peeled, seeded
  and segmented
- ½ teaspoon rose water
- 2 teaspoons orange flower water (optional)
- 4 tablespoons olive oil
- 2 teaspoons icing sugar
- 2 tablespoons chopped mint
- 1 teaspoon cinnamon
- 1 teaspoon allspice
- Salt & pepper to taste

Cook the calamari rings and tentacles
in boiling, salted water for about 5 minutes,
being careful not to overcook. They
should be tender, not tough. Remove from
water and cool.

Combine all the ingredients together in a
bowl. Serve on top of your favourite greens.

Fennel

Fennel-Calamari Salad garnished with mint sprigs.

Beets are so versatile. They can be boiled, juiced, roasted, fried, or sautéed—whatever suits your needs. The vibrant red colour looks great when they're diced and tossed into a salad. For a bright summer salad try substituting golden beets.

Red Beet Salad

serves 4

- 6 medium-sized beets
- 1 small white onion, diced
- 2 tablespoons vegetable oil for frying onion
- ⅓ cup olive or canola oil
- 3 tablespoons raspberry vinegar
- ¼ cup fresh or frozen raspberries
- 1 tablespoon chopped mint
- Salt & pepper to taste

Place beets in a pot, cover with cold water and bring to a boil. Reduce heat and cook until fork tender. Remove from the water and cool. Wearing rubber gloves so as to not stain your hands, peel and slice the beets.

Sauté the onion until translucent and add to the beets. Set aside.

Slowly stream the oil into the vinegar, whisking vigorously until a smooth mixture forms. Add the raspberries and continue to whisk until blended. Add mint, and salt and pepper to taste. Or, relax your arm muscles and put the oil, vinegar and raspberries into your blender, flip the switch and blend until smooth. Mix in the mint, salt and pepper.

Toss the beets with the raspberry dressing. Serve warm or cold.

Jaime inspires me to have fun and experiment in the kitchen. This recipe is one of my favourites to take to pot luck dinners.

This dish is best if made the day before you plan to eat it to allow the flavours to fully develop.

Curried Orange Lentil Salad

serves 6

- 1 lb orange lentils
- 1½ cups very finely chopped red onion
- 1 cup currants

Wash lentils in cold water. Place in a
pot with enough water to cover and bring
to a boil. Reduce heat and simmer until
tender, about 8–10 minutes. Rinse with cold
water and drain well. Meanwhile, prepare
the vinaigrette.

Curry Vinaigrette
- ½ cup corn oil
- ⅓ cup red wine vinegar
- 2 teaspoons salt
- 2 tablespoons sugar
- 2 teaspoons pepper
- 1 teaspoon ground cumin
- 1 teaspoon dried mustard
- ½ teaspoon turmeric
- ½ teaspoon mace
- ½ teaspoon coriander
- ½ teaspoon cardamom
- ¼ teaspoon cayenne pepper
- ¼ teaspoon nutmeg
- ¼ teaspoon cinnamon

In a large bowl, whisk together the oil,
vinegar and spices and set aside.

Combine cooked lentils with the vinaigrette.
Add onions and currants. Store in the
fridge for at least 2 hours before serving
to allow the spices to develop.

Purple rice has a naturally sweet flavour, and when paired with Asian spice, makes for an irresistible salad. The splash of dark purple adds true delight and curiosity to the dish. If purple rice is unavailable, any rice can be used.

Purple Rice Salad

serves about 6

- 3 cups of purple rice, rinsed
- 1 red pepper, diced small
- 1 yellow pepper, diced small
- 2 medium green onions
- 2 tablespoons sesame oil
- 1 tablespoon vegetable oil
- 1 tablespoon mirin (Japanese rice wine)
- 2 tablespoons tamari (or soy sauce)
- ¼ cup rice wine vinegar
- 1 tablespoon honey

Place the rice in a pot with just enough water to cover by about an inch. Add a pinch of salt and bring to a boil. Reduce heat, cover, and cook until tender, about 15 minutes. Add more hot water during the cooking process if necessary. When the rice is done, place in a bowl and let cool to room temperature.

Once the rice is cool, add the peppers and green onions. Combine the sesame oil, vegetable oil, mirin, tamari, rice wine vinegar and honey. Toss with the rice mixture. Serve. Adjust the taste with a little extra tamari if necessary.

Purple Rice Salad served with endive and garnished with yellow pepper spears.

Jaime has the art of making grain salads down to a science. This selection of recipes is just a small sampling of his grain repertoire. As Jaime always says, "experiment and have some fun with these!"

Tabbouleh makes an excellent side dish to burgers or sandwiches.

Classic Tabbouleh Salad

serves 8–10

- 2 cups bulghur wheat
- 3 lemons, juiced
- 1 cup olive oil
- 1 small red onion, chopped
- 3 small tomatoes, chopped
- 1 cucumber, peeled, seeded and diced
- 4 tablespoons fresh parsley
- 3 tablespoons chopped mint
- Salt & pepper to taste

Soak bulghur for 25 minutes in enough water to cover. Drain and squeeze any left over moisture from the grains by hand. Mix the lemon and oil until blended together and add to the bulghur. Add the remaining ingredients and let sit covered in the fridge until ready to serve. Serve cool.

Here's a slight variation to the traditional tabbouleh dish.

Minted Tabbouleh Salad with Green Apple

serves 4–6

- 2 cups water
- 1 cup uncooked bulghur wheat
- 2 tablespoons canola oil
- ½ lemon for juice (or more, to taste)
- 3 cloves garlic, whole
- Olive oil, as needed
- ½ cucumber, peeled, seeded and finely diced
- 1 small green apple, peeled, cored and diced
- ¼ cup diced tomato
- 2 tablespoons chopped mint
- Salt & pepper to taste

Boil water and add the bulghur. Return to a boil, reduce heat and cook until tender, about 8–10 minutes. Strain, cool, and squeeze out excess water. Stir in oil and lemon.

Peel the garlic and sauté in olive oil until golden. Chop. Add remaining ingredients. Serve chilled.

Israeli couscous is a large pearl-like version of the tiny bead couscous we're more used to eating. It adapts easily to different flavours and spices, and is a wonderful accompaniment to any main dish or salad.

Israeli Couscous

serves 8–10

- 1 small onion
- 3 tablespoons canola oil
- 3 cups Israeli couscous
- 4 cups vegetable stock
- 1 tablespoon chopped fresh mint
- Salt & pepper to taste

Sauté the onion in the oil. Add couscous. Cover with vegetable stock, bring to a boil and cook until tender. Add mint, salt and pepper. Fluff and serve.

Millet, a protein-rich cereal grass, has a neutral flavour that's ideal for taking on any spice or seasoning. It's very high in protein and easy to make. Quinoa, pronounced keen-wa, is grown in the Andes and is very popular in Peru. Both are readily available at natural food stores.

Millet and Quinoa Salad with Sweet Peas and Onions

serves 6–8

- 2 cups millet
- 3/4 cup quinoa
- 1 small onion, chopped
- 2 tablespoons canola oil for sauté
- 3/4 cup fresh peas (frozen okay)
- 1/2 cup tomato, diced
- 1 teaspoon salt
- 2 tablespoons chopped parsley

Combine millet and quinoa in a strainer and rinse until the water runs clear. Place in a pot with enough water to cover and bring to a boil. Lower the heat and simmer, covered, for 15 minutes. Fluff the grains with a fork to keep them from going mushy.

While the grains are cooking, sauté the onions in oil until translucent. Add peas, diced tomatoes, salt and parsley. Can be served warm or cold.

Thai Basil

These delicate appetizers are a nice light lunch dish, and are great for dipping in a variety of sauces, like, plum, sweet and sour, mustard, peanut, or tamari.

Thai Salad Rolls

makes 8–10 rolls

- 1 package rice vermicelli (or Asian noodle of your choice)
- 1 package round rice paper sheets
- 1½ cups shredded napa cabbage
- 1 large cucumber, peeled, seeded and julienned
- 1 carrot, grated
- 1 red pepper, julienned
- ¼ cup Thai basil (or Italian)
- ½ cup cilantro, chopped with stems, loosely packed
- Nori (dried seaweed) (optional)

Cook the noodles according to package directions; let cool. Fill a large skillet with warm water. Fully submerge a rice paper sheet in the water for about 15 seconds. Transfer to a flat surface and fill by arranging some noodles and cabbage in a horizontal line across the centre of the wrapper. Repeat with the carrot, pepper, cucumber, basil and cilantro. Fold the bottom of the wrapper up over the ingredients. Tuck in the sides and roll the sheet into a cylinder. Repeat until all the ingredients and wrappers have been used up. For a garnish, place a strip of seaweed along the centre.

Cilantro

Polenta, which is made of cornmeal, can be grilled, fried, sautéed, or roasted, served as a main course, appetizer or side dish. The sweet flavour of corn blends well with vegetables, nuts, cheese and fruit. This recipe is for firm polenta, which is ideal for roasting, grilling or frying. It can be made a day ahead and kept in the fridge until ready to use. Top with fresh cheese and sautéed spinach or grilled vegetables.

Polenta

serves 10

- 12 cups water
- 2½ teaspoons salt
- 1 teaspoon butter
- 3 tablespoons olive oil
- 3½ cups (1lb) cornmeal
- ½ cup grated parmesan cheese

Bring the water to a roaring boil. Add the salt, butter and olive oil. With a wire whisk, stir the water into a whirlpool. Slowly sprinkle in the cornmeal. Keep stirring in the same direction until all the cornmeal is added and there are no lumps.

Reduce the heat to low and cover the pot with foil. Cook 45 minutes to an hour, stirring occasionally with a wooden spoon. When done, add the grated cheese. Pour the polenta into a buttered or sprayed 9 x 13 inch cooking pan. Allow to cool.

Hint: Be sure to wear long sleeves to protect your arms, because the bubbles will spit just like a hot, simmering tomato sauce.

Life on the road is fun, but it can be
very challenging both mentally and physically.
Eating right and getting lots of exercise
become very important for all of us
so that we can look and feel our best.

Sometimes after a show we'll all be hungry. But instead of eating a heavy meal like pizza, we'll often eat sushi that Jaime prepares for us. It's a nice light snack that leaves you feeling satisfied but not stuffed.

Nori, which is dried seaweed, can be filled with whatever you like, from fresh mangoes to multi-coloured peppers. Rolling sushi is easy once you get the hang of it. Sushi rollers, which are small bamboo mats, are available in most Asian marketplaces and some grocery stores. Serve with wasabi, a hot Japanese horseradish.

Veggie Sushi
serves 4–6

Rice

- 1 cup short grain rice
- ½ cup rice vinegar
- 3 tablespoons sugar
- 1 teaspoon salt

Filling

- 2 ripe avocados, cut into strips
- 1 large carrot, julienned
- 1 large cucumber, julienned
- Mirin (Japanese rice wine) (optional)
- 1 package toasted nori (about 10 sheets)

Wash the rice in a strainer until the water runs clear. Place in a pot with enough water to cover by 1 inch. Bring to a boil and reduce the heat, cooking until tender. During cooking the rice can be gently broken apart so it doesn't stick together. Allow the rice to cool. Add the vinegar, sugar and salt and stir gently.

Soak the avocados, carrot and cucumber in just enough rice wine to cover.

Place a piece of nori on the sushi roller. Spread a thin layer of rice over the sheet, to ¼ inch from the edges. Place the ingredients in the centre of the rice and roll nori into a cylinder. Carefully seal with a bit of rice vinegar. Wrap the finished roll in plastic wrap and refrigerate until ready to use.

With a sharp, wet knife, cut the sushi about ½ an inch thick. Serve with soy sauce, pickled ginger and wasabi.

When we're *on the road* we try to surround ourselves with as many *elements from home* as possible.

Our dog, Rex, who we love very much, goes everywhere we go—we'd *miss her* too much otherwise! She *brings us so much joy* and keeps us grounded in reality.

This simple recipe is great served with stir-fried vegetables. It uses silken tofu, which can be found in the dairy or vegetable section of most grocery stores.

Deep-Fried Tofu

serves 2

Tofu
- 1 block silken tofu
- 4 tablespoons cornstarch
- Vegetable oil for deep-frying

Carefully remove the tofu from the package and wrap in cheese cloth. Refrigerate for 30 minutes. Cut the tofu into cubes.

Heat the oil to about 350°F

Gently coat the tofu with cornstarch and deep-fry until golden brown and crispy, about 5–6 minutes. If you're using a frying pan instead of a deep-fryer, the tofu can be gently turned until it's browned on all sides.

Remove from the oil and drain on paper towel. Serve with the following sauce.

Dipping Sauce
- 1 tablespoon saki rice wine
- 4 tablespoons mirin (Japanese rice wine)
- 2 tablespoons tamari (or soy sauce)
- 1 teaspoon rice vinegar
- 1 green onion, sliced

Mix ingredients together right before serving the tofu.

Samosas

makes 30 Samosas

- 2 large boiling potatoes
- 1/2 teaspoon toasted mustard seeds
- 1 cup green peas (fresh or frozen)
- 1/2 teaspoon lemon juice
- 1 teaspoon molasses
- 1 teaspoon honey
- 3 tablespoons chopped cilantro
- 1/2 teaspoon paprika
- 1 pinch chili flakes
- Salt and pepper to taste
- 12 phyllo dough sheets (or frozen samosa or puff pastry dough)
- Melted butter as needed, about 1/4 cup

Preheat oven to 375°F

Peel and dice the potatoes and cook until tender. Toast the mustard seeds in a small pan just until golden brown. Steam or parboil the peas.

Mix potatoes, mustard seeds, peas, lemon juice, molasses, honey and cilantro together with the spices in a bowl. Season with salt and pepper to taste.

Set the phyllo sheets to one side and keep them covered with a damp towel as you work.

Working with one sheet at a time, brush the first sheet of phyllo lightly with some of the melted butter. Place a second sheet on top and brush with butter; repeat a third time. Cut into long strips about 3 inches wide. Place about a tablespoon of filling at the end of each strip. Fold one corner of the strip up and over the filling, then continue to fold the strip loosely to form a neat triangle. Crimp the edges and brush again with melted butter.

Bake for 35–45 minutes or until golden brown.

29

Spicy Spring Rolls

makes 12 rolls

Cilantro

Savoy Cabbage

- 3 tablespoons chopped ginger
- 2 tablespoons chopped garlic
- 3 tablespoons chopped green onion
- 1 tablespoon hot bean paste
  or red chili paste
- 1 tablespoon vegetable oil
- 1 cup fresh bean sprouts
- 1 cup grated carrot
- 1 cup finely sliced savoy cabbage
- 1 red pepper, julienned
- 5 shiitake mushrooms, julienned
- 3 tablespoons mirin (Japanese rice wine)
- 1 tablespoon hoisin sauce
- ¼ cup soy sauce
- 12 spring roll wrappers
- 1 cup peeled, grated cucumber
- 3 tablespoons chopped cilantro
- Oil for frying

In a very hot wok briefly sauté the ginger, garlic, green onion and chili paste in the oil. Add the bean sprouts, carrots, savoy cabbage, red pepper and mushrooms and cook at high heat until the vegetables begin to soften. Add the mirin, hoisin sauce and soy sauce. Remove from heat and let cool in a bowl at room temperature.

Place the spring roll wrappers under a damp cloth to keep them moist. Place wrappers one at a time on a hard surface with one corner pointing towards you. Spoon cooled ingredients into the centre. Add a tablespoon of grated cucumber and a sprinkle of cilantro.

Fold the side corners into the centre. Fold the bottom into the centre, making sure the three corners are touching each other. To finish, roll the wrapper away from you and up over the final corner. Store rolls under a damp cloth until ready to fry.

Heat enough oil to cover the rolls, and fry seam side down until golden brown. Drain on paper towel and serve with your favourite dipping sauce.

Serve dipping sauces in sake cups for an interesting look.

This soup has a rich, thick texture, yet it's very low in fat.

Hearty Potato-Leek Soup

serves 4–6

- $\frac{1}{2}$ lb leeks, julienned
- 3 tablespoons vegetable oil
- $4\frac{1}{2}$ cups vegetable stock
- 1 bay leaf
- 1 garlic clove, minced
- 1 lb large baking potatoes, peeled and diced
- $\frac{1}{2}$ cup low-fat milk, heated
- Salt and white pepper to taste
- Pinch of nutmeg
- $\frac{3}{4}$ teaspoon chopped fresh chives

In a large pot, sauté leeks in vegetable oil until tender. Add 1 cup of stock, bay leaf, and garlic. Cover and cook for 10 minutes. Add the remaining stock and bring to a boil. Add potatoes and cook until tender, about 20 minutes. Remove bay leaf and puree the potatoes. Stir in milk, reduce heat to a simmer and cook an additional 5 minutes. Season with salt, pepper, and a pinch of nutmeg. Garnish with fresh chopped chives.

This is a very flavourful, hearty soup.

Creamy Mushroom-Sherry Soup

serves 6

- 4 cups low-fat milk
- 1 lb assorted mushrooms, sliced
- 3 tablespoons chopped garlic
- Vegetable oil for sauté
- ½ cup cooking sherry
- 3 tablespoons chopped parsley
- 3 tablespoons vegetable oil
- 6 tablespoons butter
- 1 large onion, diced
- ½ cup flour
- Salt & pepper to taste

Warm the milk in a heavy saucepan over low heat. Meanwhile, sauté mushrooms and garlic in vegetable oil until golden brown. Add the sherry and parsley and set aside.

In a large soup pot, sauté the onions in vegetable oil and butter until translucent. Add flour and cook for about a minute. Gradually whisk in the warm milk and bring to a simmer. Do not boil. Once thickened, add the sautéed mushroom and sherry mixture. Reduce the heat and allow to thicken completely, stirring often.

Garnish with parsley, season with salt and pepper and if you like, add a bit more sherry.

Curried Split Pea Soup

serves 6

- 1 small onion, diced
- 1 small leek, diced
- 3 cloves garlic, chopped
- 2 tablespoons butter or oil
- 1 teaspoon curry powder
- 1 teaspoon turmeric
- 1 tablespoon tomato paste
- 1 tablespoon vinegar
- ½ cup carrots, peeled and chopped
- ½ cup celery, peeled and chopped
- 6 cups yellow peas, rinsed well
- 8 cups vegetable stock
- 1 bay leaf

- 1 tablespoon fresh thyme
- ½ teaspoon caraway seeds
- 1 teaspoon mustard seeds (toast in
  a hot dry sauté pan)

In a soup pot, sauté the onions, leeks and garlic in the butter or oil over medium heat for about 3 minutes. Add curry powder and turmeric and continue cooking until the onions are translucent. Add the tomato paste and cook for 1 minute. Add the vinegar, carrots, celery, peas, vegetable stock, bay leaf, thyme, caraway and mustard seeds.

Bring to a boil, reduce heat and simmer, stirring often, until the peas are tender, about 45 minutes. Remove the bay leaf.

Puree the soup with a hand blender. For a real treat, garnish with toasted mustard seeds and a bit of spiced curry oil. To make curry oil, simply mix a bit of curry with some oil.

Minted Split Pea Soup with Caramelized Shallots

serves 6

- 1 large onion, chopped
- 2 celery stalks, finely chopped
- 2 tablespoons butter or oil
- 6 cups split peas, rinsed
- 8 cups vegetable stock
- 1 bay leaf
- 1 tablespoon liquid smoke
- 3 large potatoes, peeled and cubed
- 6 shallots, very thinly sliced (optional)
- 1 tablespoon butter
- 3 tablespoons canola or olive oil
- 3 tablespoons chopped mint
- Salt & pepper to taste

In a soup pot, lightly heat the onions and celery in the butter until just softened. Add the peas, stock, bay leaf, liquid smoke and potatoes. Bring to a boil, reduce heat and simmer for about 45 minutes.

Meanwhile, melt butter with the oil over low heat. Add shallots and cook slowly until golden brown. Set aside.

When the soup is done remove the bay leaf. Puree if necessary. Add mint, salt and pepper to taste. Top with caramelized shallots.

Shallots

Jaime prepares food for up to 100 people three times a day. He's *up at five* and in bed *after midnight,* yet somehow he still manages to make every meal *a visual and taste sensation.*

Miso is a very flavourful paste made from steamed soybeans, which are then blended with wheat, rice and sea salt and fermented. Aside from soup, miso can be used in gravies, and salad dressings, or when broiling fish.

Miso Soup

serves 4

- 1 cup shiitake mushrooms
- 1 small leek
- ½ lb tofu
- 4 cups vegetable stock
- ½ cup red miso paste
- Nori (dried seaweed) for garnish (optional)

If using dried shiitake mushrooms, soak in water 30 minutes and drain. Remove any tough stems. Slice the leek width-wise into ½ inch pieces. Cut tofu into ½ inch cubes. Heat the vegetable stock in a pot over low heat; add the miso paste and bring to a boil. Lower heat to a simmer. Add the leeks, mushrooms and tofu and heat through. Garnish with strips of seaweed and serve.

This soup can be made with or without cream. The full cream version gives the soup a rich, velvety finish.

Gingered Butternut Squash Soup

serves 6–8

- 3 medium-sized butternut squash
- 2 tablespoons vegetable oil
- 1 medium onion, diced
- 2 cloves garlic, chopped
- 2 tablespoons chopped ginger
- 1 teaspoon allspice
- ½ teaspoon cinnamon
- ½ teaspoon Old Bay seasoning (optional)
- 6 cups vegetable stock
- ½ cup simmered heavy cream (optional)
- Salt & pepper to taste

Preheat oven to 375 F

Cut the butternut squash in half lengthwise and clean out the seeds. Place sliced side down on a lightly oiled baking sheet. Cover with foil and bake until tender, about 30 minutes.

Heat the oil and sauté the onion, garlic, ginger and spices until the onion is translucent. Add the stock and bring to a boil.

Scoop out the cooked squash and add to the soup. Puree the ingredients with a hand blender. Add the warm, simmered cream now, if you like. Season with salt and pepper.

Shiitake Soup with a Puff Pastry Lid

serves 4

Ginger

Savoy Cabbage

Preheat oven to 400°F

- 12 shiitake mushrooms
- ½ cup flour
- 1 sheet puff pastry
- 2 cloves garlic, chopped
- 2 tablespoons chopped ginger
- 2 tablespoons sesame oil
- 1 head savoy cabbage, thinly sliced, stalk removed
- 1 small carrot, peeled and julienned
- 1 tablespoon red miso
- 2 tablespoons soy sauce
- Hot bean paste to taste
- 6 cups vegetable stock
- 1 green onion, thinly sliced
- ¼ lb firm silken tofu, cubed
- 1-8 oz can sliced water chestnuts, drained
- Eggwash (two egg yolks, beaten)

If using dried shiitake mushrooms, soak for 30 minutes in enough hot water to cover. Set aside.

Lay the puff pastry sheet on a floured work surface and roll out to about ⅛ inch thick. Cut into four equal squares. Put on a plate and refrigerate until needed.

Drain the shiitake mushrooms. Remove the stems and discard. Slice. In a soup pot, sauté the garlic and ginger in oil for 1 minute. Add cabbage, carrots and mushrooms and cook until almost tender. Add miso, soy sauce, hot bean paste and stock. Bring to a boil, then turn off heat. Add green onion, tofu and water chestnuts.

Ladle the soup into four oven-safe bowls. Brush the edges and top lip of the bowls with eggwash. Cover each bowl with pastry and brush with remaining eggwash. Bake until golden brown, about 10 minutes.

Curried Corn Chowder

serves 10–12

- 2 cups corn kernels, roasted
- $\frac{1}{2}$ cup chopped white onion
- 4 tablespoons corn oil
- 1 teaspoon garam masala
- $\frac{1}{4}$ teaspoon turmeric
- $\frac{1}{4}$ teaspoon nutmeg
- $\frac{1}{4}$ teaspoon curry powder
- 1 tablespoon curry paste
- 4 cups unroasted corn kernels
- 8 cups vegetable stock
- 2 tablespoons chopped garlic
- 2 tablespoons chopped ginger
- $\frac{1}{4}$ cup diced red pepper
- $\frac{1}{4}$ cup diced yellow pepper
- $\frac{1}{4}$ cup diced green pepper
- $\frac{1}{2}$ cup chopped and loosely
  packed cilantro
- Salt & pepper to taste

Preheat oven to 375°F

To roast corn, place 2 cups corn on a baking sheet with a little bit of vegetable oil and roast for about 8 minutes or until golden brown. Set aside.

In a soup pot, sauté the onion in corn oil until translucent. Add the spices and curry paste. Stir. Add the unroasted corn and vegetable stock. Cook 15–20 minutes. Puree with a hand blender until smooth.

In a separate sauté pan, sauté the garlic and ginger. Add the peppers and sauté until tender. Add to the soup pot along with the cilantro and roasted corn. Season with salt and pepper. Serve.

Sometimes I feel like
I'm living two very separate lives.
As much as I love *touring and performing,*
I'm a *homebody at heart.*

Jaime was one of eleven children. He often tells me that his mom and sisters inspired him to become a chef. This recipe comes from one of his sisters. I can see why he was inspired!

Cookie's Stuffed Mushrooms

serves 6

- 12 large mushroom caps
- Olive oil, as needed
- 2 medium onions, diced
- 5 cloves garlic, chopped
- ½ cup white wine
- 1 cup seasoned bread crumbs
- 3 tablespoons parsley
- ½ cup grated parmesan
  or pecorino cheese
- Salt & pepper to taste
- 12 chips of butter

Preheat the oven to 350°F

Remove mushroom stems and set aside. With a melon baller, hollow out the mushroom caps and reserve the innards. Place caps on a lightly oiled cookie sheet.

Finely chop the mushroom stems and innards. Sauté onion and garlic on low heat until translucent. Add chopped mushrooms, raise the heat and cook for 5 minutes. Add white wine and cook until the liquid is almost evaporated. Add bread crumbs and parsley. Allow to cool; add grated cheese and a little olive oil or water until mixture achieves a clay-like consistency. The mixture should be moist, not wet. Season to taste.

Fill the mushroom caps. Place a small dollop of butter on top of each mushroom and bake for 20 minutes or until golden brown.

Entrées

Yellow Bell Pepper

This easy recipe is great if you're cooking for a crowd of people. Vary the vegetables according to what's in season, or simply include your own favourite vegetables. It's great served with garlic aioli, which should be made ahead of time.

It's a Wrap

serves 4–6

Preheat oven to 350°F

- 2 cloves garlic, chopped
- 1 small onion, chopped
- 1 each of green, yellow and red pepper, sliced in strips
- 1 small zucchini, sliced in strips
- 1 small eggplant, sliced in strips
- 1 tomato, sliced in strips
- 3 tablespoons olive oil
- 2 tablespoons balsamic vinegar
- 2 tablespoons chopped fresh thyme
- 1 teaspoon salt
- Freshly ground pepper to taste
- 1 cup long grain white rice, cooked
- 1 cup shredded low-fat mozzarella
- 4–6 large burrito wrappers (flavoured are the best)

Mix the vegetables together with the oil, vinegar, thyme, salt and pepper and place on a baking sheet. Cover with foil and bake for 30 minutes.

Prepare rice according to package directions. Fill the wraps with the roasted vegetables, rice and grated cheese. Roll and enjoy. Serve with garlic aioli.

Aioli
- 2 roasted garlic cloves mashed into a paste
- 1 egg yolk
- 1/2 tablespoon water
- 1/2 teaspoon dry mustard
- 1/2 cup canola or vegetable oil
- 1/2 cup olive oil
- 1/2 tablespoon red or white wine vinegar
- Salt and pepper
- Lemon juice to taste

Preheat oven to 350°F

Wrap unpeeled garlic cloves in aluminum foil and bake until they pop out of the skin easily, about 15 minutes. Remove the skin and mash cloves into a paste.

Whip the egg yolk, water and mustard together with a hand mixer or whisk until foamy. Slowly add oil, whisking constantly, until thick. Add roasted garlic, vinegar, salt, pepper, and a squeeze of lemon juice. Cover and refrigerate until ready to use.

Japanese Eggplant

I first *fell in love* with our house because
of *the wonderful* old-style *stove.*

The kitchen is the room *we spend
the most time* in—it's the *heart*
and *soul of our home.*
(I think this is the first time all six elements
were used at once!)

This hearty chili calls for seitan, an excellent meat substitute made from wheat gluten. Seitan, or "wheat meat," can be found in most Asian markets and health food stores.

Vegetarian Chili

serves 8–10

Ash in the wine cellar

- 1 large onion, chopped
- 4 cloves garlic, chopped
- 3 tablespoons olive oil
- 1 teaspoon turmeric
- 1 teaspoon cumin
- 1 tablespoon chili powder
- 1 teaspoon dry mustard
- ½ teaspoon cayenne pepper
- 1 small red pepper, diced
- 1 small green pepper, diced
- 1 small orange pepper, diced (optional)
- 4 tomatoes, peeled and chopped
- 1½ cups canned white navy beans, drained
- 1½ cups canned kidney beans, drained
- 1½ cups canned black beans, drained
- 1 cup corn kernels
- ¾ cup green peas
- 1 cup ground seitan
- 1 cup firm tofu, drained and cubed
- ½ cup chopped cilantro or parsley
- Water or tomato juice as needed
- Salt and freshly ground pepper
- Shredded cheddar cheese

Sauté onions and garlic in oil until translucent. Add turmeric, cumin, chili powder, dry mustard and cayenne. Cook for about a minute. Add peppers and cook until tender. Add tomatoes, beans, corn, peas and seitan. Simmer for about 30 minutes, stirring occasionally. If the mixture becomes too dry add some tomato juice or water. Right before serving, add tofu and cilantro or parsley. Season with salt and pepper. Garnish with cheese.

For a real treat serve with minted yogurt, which is simply plain yogurt mixed with a bit of chopped mint.

These quick recipes are versatile enough to be served at any mealtime.

Asparagus Frittata

serves 4–6

Portobello Mushrooms

Preheat oven to 350°F

- 5 stalks fresh asparagus
- 8 eggs, beaten
- ¼ cup milk
- ⅛ teaspoon ground nutmeg
- Salt and pepper to taste
- 1 medium onion, sliced
- Vegetable oil for cooking
- 6 button mushrooms, sliced
- 1 cup chopped fresh spinach
- 2 chopped tomatoes, roma or plum
- ¼ lb shredded mozzarella
- 1 small bunch chopped basil

Remove the tough ends of the asparagus and discard. Blanch or steam asparagus for 5 minutes or until bright green and tender. Rinse under cold water and drain thoroughly.

Beat eggs and milk together. Season with nutmeg, salt and pepper; set aside.

In a cast iron skillet, sauté onion in oil until translucent. Add mushrooms and sauté until golden brown. Add spinach and cook until completely wilted. Add chopped tomatoes. Pour egg mixture into skillet; stir briefly. Sprinkle mozzarella on top, decorate with asparagus and basil and bake 10–15 minutes or until cheese is melted and bubbly.

Baked Italian Vegetable Frittata

serves 4–6

Peppers

Preheat oven to 350°F

- 1 large onion, thinly sliced
- 6 cloves garlic, chopped
- ¼ cup olive oil
- ¼ cup chopped fresh parsley
- 2 sprigs rosemary, finely chopped
- 1 sprig fresh thyme, finely chopped
- 1 small zucchini, thinly sliced
- 2 plum tomatoes, seeded and diced
- 1 portobello mushroom, diced
- 1 green pepper, julienned
- 1 red pepper, julienned
- 10 eggs, beaten
- ½ cup cubed asiago cheese
- 4 tablespoons parmesan cheese

Sauté onion and garlic in olive oil until translucent. Add parsley, rosemary, thyme and vegetables; sauté until tender. Remove from heat and cool. Mix vegetables, asiago, parmesan and eggs together. Pour into a greased 9 x 13 inch baking pan; bake 20–25 minutes or until the top browns.

While on the Lilith Fair tour my schedule was so hectic that sometimes I didn't get a chance to eat before running off to a press conference. Jaime would whip up something like this dish in a matter of minutes.

This simple, versatile brunch-type omelette only takes a few minutes to prepare. Add different cooked veggies, or even leftover burrito filling. This recipe calls for peppered jack cheese, but any cheese can be used.

Wild Asparagus Omelette with Peppered Jack Cheese and Chipotle Sour Cream

serves 2

- 1 lb asparagus
- 5 eggs, beaten
- ¼ cup peppered jack cheese
- Salt & pepper to taste
- Olive oil
- 1 cup low-fat sour cream
- 1 small chipotle pepper

Remove the tough ends of the asparagus and discard. Blanch or steam for 5 minutes or until bright green and tender. Rinse under cold water and drain thoroughly.

Beat the eggs, then gently add the asparagus, cheese, and a pinch of salt and pepper. Heat the olive oil in a skillet and add the egg mixture. Cook just until the bottom solidifies; flip over and cook the other side.

Mix sour cream and chipotle peppers together and spread on top. Serve warm.

Lilith Fair is a summer music festival that I helped to *establish celebrating* the *amazing diversity* in *music* made by *women today.*
This shot was taken the first year—1997.

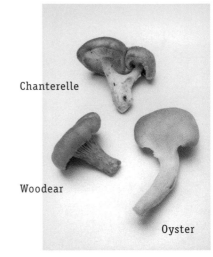

Chanterelle

Woodear

Oyster

This very simple dish will turn out perfectly every time simply by following a few guidelines. First, always use a heavy-bottomed skillet. Second, add the stock to the arborio rice a little at a time. Finally, the stock should be kept hot.

Wild Mushroom Risotto with Asparagus

Serves 4–6

- 3 tablespoons olive oil
- 2 cloves garlic, chopped
- A sprig of rosemary
- 2 cups assorted mushrooms, such as chanterelle, button or black trumpet, sliced
- Salt and pepper
- 9 asparagus stalks
- 6 cups vegetable stock
- 2 tablespoons unsalted butter
- 1 tablespoon olive oil
- 1 medium onion, finely diced
- 2 cups arborio rice
- 1/3 cup dry white wine, warmed
- Salt and freshly ground white pepper
- 1 tablespoon butter
- 2/3 to 1 cup parmesan cheese

Sauté the garlic, rosemary and mushrooms until golden brown. Season with salt and pepper and set aside. Remove the rosemary.

Remove the tough ends of the asparagus and discard. Blanch or steam for 5 minutes, or until bright green and tender. Rinse under cold water and drain thoroughly. Cut into thirds and set aside.

Bring vegetable stock to a slow simmer and keep over low heat. Meanwhile, in a heavy saucepan, melt the butter over medium heat. Add olive oil and onion and sauté until translucent. Add rice and gently stir with a wooden spoon, using broad strokes in a figure eight pattern to sweep up the rice from the bottom of the pot. Cook for 4–5 minutes until rice begins to look chalky. Add warmed white wine and stir until almost completely absorbed. Add hot stock one cup at a time, stirring until liquid is almost completely absorbed before adding more stock. Continue until all the hot stock is used up. When done the rice should be creamy and tender—al dente or "to the tooth," but not soft or mushy. Remove from heat and gently fold in cooked asparagus and mushroom mixture. With the same light touch, stir in the butter and grated cheese.

Buon Appetito!

This dish calls for Thai basil, but Italian basil can also be used. Also used are dried kaffir lime leaves. Each leaf has a unique double shape and looks like two leaves joined end to end. Both items can usually be found at Asian markets.

Squash Curry
serves 6

- 4 acorn squash
- ¼ cup vegetable oil
- 1 small onion, chopped
- 1 leek, sliced
- 10 cloves garlic, crushed and chopped
- ¼ cup shredded ginger
- 1 tablespoon red curry paste
- 6 kaffir lime leaves
- 1 green pepper, chopped
- 1 red pepper, chopped
- 1 medium Japanese eggplant, sliced
- ½ lb button mushrooms, chopped
- 2 medium tomatoes, chopped
- ¼ lb okra, stems removed, sliced
- 1-14 oz can chick peas, drained
- 1½ cups green peas
- ½ cup torn Thai basil
- ½ cup shredded Italian basil
- ½ cup chopped tarragon
- 1 tablespoon curry powder
- 1 teaspoon turmeric
- 1 teaspoon toasted mustard seeds
- 1½ cups coconut milk
- 1 cup vegetable stock

Preheat oven to 350°F

Split the squash in half and scoop out the seeds. Rub the sliced edges with a small amount of vegetable oil and season with salt and pepper. Place cut side down on a baking sheet, cover with foil and bake for 30 minutes or until tender.

In a soup pot, sauté the onions, leeks, garlic, and ginger until aromatic and lightly golden. Add the curry paste and cook for two minutes.

Tear each lime leaf in half and add to the pot. Add peppers, eggplant and mushrooms and cook for 4–5 minutes. Add tomatoes, okra, chick peas, peas, herbs, spices and coconut milk. Cook 10 minutes. Add the vegetable stock in intervals until a stew-like consistency is reached.

Scoop out the tender insides of 1 whole squash and add it to the stew. To serve the curry, use the other cooked halves as bowls.

This dish was inspired by the classic French apple tart tatin, which is made upside down and flipped over to serve. The dish starts on top of the stove and finishes in the oven, so you'll need an oven friendly sauté pan. This savoury version is served with balsamic whipped cream.

Mushroom Tart Tatin

serves 2

- ⅓ cup balsamic vinegar
- A handful of flour
- 1 sheet of puff pastry, thawed
- 1 small yellow onion, sliced
- 3 garlic cloves, chopped
- 3 tablespoons olive oil
- 1 cup assorted mushrooms, sliced
- 4 ripe cherry tomatoes, halved
- 5 fresh basil leaves, shredded
- Salt and pepper to taste
- ½ cup whipping cream

Preheat oven to 350°F

Reduce balsamic vinegar over high heat until it reaches a syrup-like consistency. Remove from heat and test by putting a dot of the vinegar on a white plate. It should be thick like molasses and very dark in colour. Put back on heat if necessary, being very careful not to burn it. When finished set aside.

Dust a work surface with flour. Roll pastry dough into a ⅛ inch thick circle, starting from the centre of the dough and working towards the edge. Place a sauté pan upside-down on the dough and trace around it with a small knife. The resulting circle will fit perfectly in the pan. Refrigerate until needed.

In the same sauté pan, sauté the onions and garlic in oil, being careful not to brown the garlic. Add mushrooms and sauté until golden brown. Add tomato and basil and season with salt and pepper.

Place the pastry circle on top of the mushrooms and poke a few holes in it to let the steam escape. Continue to cook until the pastry starts to sweat. Remove from heat and place in the oven; bake until golden brown, about 10–15 minutes.

Meanwhile, whip the cream until stiff peaks form. Stir in one half of the reduced balsamic vinegar.

To serve; using oven mitts, place an inverted plate on top of the pan and carefully and quickly flip the pan over so the mushrooms are on top. Top with balsamic whipped cream just before serving. Drizzle the remaining balsamic vinegar over the top.

Here are two more of Jaime's family recipes.
Both of these rustic pastas are great on a cold rainy day when you need something to warm you up.

Nettie's Pasta Piselli

serves about 6–8 hungry people

- 16 oz tubetti pasta (or any small pasta)
- 1 large white onion, chopped
- 3 cloves garlic, finely chopped
- 2 sprigs rosemary
- 5 cups green peas
- 3 roma tomatoes, diced small
- 6 cups vegetable stock
- Olive oil to taste
- ½ cup parmesan cheese
- Salt & pepper to taste

Cook pasta according to package directions. Meanwhile, in a large pot, sauté onions, garlic and rosemary in olive oil until the onions become translucent. Add the peas and tomatoes; toss gently. Add stock and bring to a boil. Cook for about 6 minutes, then add hot pasta. Remove rosemary; season to taste. Ladle into bowls, sprinkle with parmesan, and if desired, drizzle with a bit of olive oil.

Dina's Pasta 'n' Potatoes

serves 4–6

- 1 lb any small pasta
- 1 large onion, chopped
- 6 cloves crushed (not chopped) garlic
- Pinch of chili flakes
- ¼ cup olive oil
- 1 bunch fresh oregano, chopped
- 5 medium white potatoes, diced
- 3 cups vegetable stock
- 5 roma tomatoes, chopped
- ½ cup chopped chunky parmesan cheese
- Olive oil to taste
- Salt & pepper to taste

Prepare pasta according to package directions, *al dente* style. Meanwhile, in a medium-sized pot, sauté onion, garlic and chili flakes in olive oil until tender. Add oregano, potatoes and stock. Cook until potatoes are barely tender; add tomatoes. Continue cooking until potatoes are done. Remove half of the soup and puree with a hand blender. Pour back into the pot and cook for 1 minute. Adjust the thickness with extra stock if necessary. Add pasta and cheese; garnish with additional chopped oregano and, if desired, drizzle with olive oil before serving.

59

This warm, creamy pasta dish can be served mild or spicy. Pass the hot sauce at the table.
Farfalle pasta, which is shaped like butterflies or bow-ties, can be found at most grocery stores.

Smoky Pablano Pasta with Black Bean and Roasted Corn Cream Sauce

serves 4

- 1 large pablano pepper
- 2 cups corn kernels
- 3 cups heavy cream
- 1 medium onion, diced
- 3 cloves garlic, chopped
- 1 stalk celery, finely chopped
- 2 tablespoons vegetable oil
- 1 red pepper, diced
- 1 yellow pepper, diced
- 1 heaping tablespoon all-purpose flour
- 1-14 oz can black beans, rinsed
- 1 large tomato, diced
- 2 tablespoons liquid smoke
- 4 tablespoons chopped cilantro
- Salt & pepper to taste
- 1 lb farfalle pasta

Preheat oven to 375°F

Bake whole pablano pepper and corn on a lightly oiled baking sheet, keeping the two separate, until the skin of the pepper is browned and the corn is golden coloured. Place roasted pepper in a bowl, cover with plastic wrap, and let sit for 10 minutes. Remove skin and seeds, chop pepper and set aside.

Cook pasta according to package directions. Meanwhile, warm the cream in a small pot. In a separate pot sauté onion, garlic, and celery in oil until soft. Add red and yellow peppers; cook until tender. Add flour and stir. Add warm cream one ladle at a time, stirring constantly. Bring to a boil. Add the black beans, diced tomato, liquid smoke and cilantro. Season with salt and pepper. Stir in pablano peppers and roasted corn. Continue to cook the sauce until it smoothly coats the back of a spoon. Drain pasta and toss with the cream sauce.

Jaime is a *patient guide* when teaching others.
I like to turn the burners on full and I sometimes
burn whatever I'm doing and have to start again.
A few helpful hints go a long way...

Fresh rice noodles are often a challenge to find, so you can substitute dried noodles if you like. Prepare the ingredients ahead of time and stir-fry just before serving.

Thai Rice Noodle and Vegetable Stir-Fry

serves 4–6

Thai Eggplant

Lemon Grass

- 1 lb fresh thick rice noodles
- 1 tablespoon vegetable oil
- 3 tablespoons vegetable or wok oil
- 2 cloves garlic, chopped
- 1 tablespoon chopped ginger
- 1 tablespoon chopped lemon grass
- 1 tablespoon red curry paste
- 8 green onions, sliced
- 6 Thai eggplants, chopped
- 1 red pepper, sliced
- 1 green pepper, sliced
- 1 small can bamboo shoots
- 1/2 lb firm tofu, cubed
- 3/4 cup coconut milk
- 1 tablespoon fish sauce

Place noodles in a heat-safe bowl and cover with boiling water. Let stand for 10 minutes. Drain well, and toss with 1 tablespoon of oil. Set aside.

In a hot wok or large sauté pan, cook the garlic, ginger, lemon grass, curry paste and green onions until the onions become tender. Add eggplant and peppers and cook until they begin to release their juices, about 3 minutes. Add bamboo shoots and tofu and cook another 2 minutes. Add coconut milk and fish sauce and bring to a boil. Add the rice noodles, heat through, and serve.

To decorate the serving dish, try cutting out different pepper shapes and arranging them on the plate.

When a meal is prepared with *care and love* I truly believe it makes the *food taste better* —service with a smile always helps!

This recipe calls for reducing balsamic vinegar down into a syrup, so it's a bit more challenging to make than others. However, the resulting flavour is well worth the extra effort.

Penne Pasta in Balsamic Cream with Caramelized Shallots

serves 4–6

- 4 cups heavy cream
- A sprig of rosemary
- 2 cups balsamic vinegar
- 1 tablespoon butter
- 3 tablespoons canola or olive oil
- 10 shallots, very thinly sliced
- 1 lb penne pasta
- 2 cloves garlic, chopped
- 4 roma tomatoes, seeded and diced
- 5 large basil leaves, sliced into thin strips
- 4 tablespoons parmesan cheese

Reduce cream and rosemary in a heavy saucepan over high heat until thick. Remove rosemary and discard. Meanwhile, in another pot reduce the balsamic vinegar over high heat until it reaches a syrup-like consistency. Remove from heat and test by putting a dot of the vinegar on a white plate. It should be thick like molasses and very dark in colour. Put back on heat if necessary, being very careful not to burn it. Set aside.

Melt butter with the oil over low heat. Add shallots and cook slowly until golden brown. Remove from pan and set aside.

Cook penne according to package directions and drain. Meanwhile, in a large pot sauté garlic in a bit of oil over medium heat. Add reduced cream and cook about 20 seconds. Add the cooked pasta, making sure it's completely coated in cream. Add the diced tomatoes, heating through for about a minute. Remove from heat and stir in reduced balsamic vinegar, fresh basil, and parmesan cheese. Top with caramelized shallots and serve.

Cannelloni is a classic Italian dish, baked casserole style. It's great to make on a lazy Sunday when you have the time to prepare it. This recipe calls for store bought fresh pasta sheets, but you can make your own or use dried packaged cannelloni. The sauce can be made a day in advance for quick assembly the next day.

Spinach and Pine Nut Cannelloni

serves 6

Bechamel Sauce

- 1 cup whole milk
- 1½ tablespoons unsalted butter
- 2 tablespoons + ¾ teaspoon flour
- ⅛ teaspoon ground nutmeg
- Salt & pepper to taste

Scald the milk in a small saucepan. Meanwhile, melt butter over medium heat in a heavy-bottomed sauce pan. Add flour and stir until combined. Gradually add hot milk and cook over low heat, stirring constantly until thickened. Add nutmeg, season to taste, and set aside.

Tomato Sauce

- 1-28 oz can whole tomatoes
- 1 medium onion, chopped
- 2 tablespoons olive oil
- 3 cloves garlic, minced
- ¼ cup minced Italian parsley
- 1 cup warm bechamel sauce
- Salt and pepper to taste

Drain and crush the tomatoes. Set aside. Sauté onions in oil until translucent. Add garlic, parsley and tomatoes and cook over medium heat for about 10 minutes, stirring occasionally. Add the warm bechamel, heat to boiling, remove from heat and cover.

Cannelloni

- ½ cup toasted pine nuts, finely chopped
- 1 medium onion, finely chopped
- 2 tablespoons olive oil
- 2 cloves garlic, minced
- 2 cups frozen spinach, thawed and drained or 1 lb fresh, washed and chopped
- ½ cup dry white wine (or vegetable stock)
- 1 cup bread crumbs
- 1½ cups ricotta cheese
- 1 egg, beaten (optional)
- 2 tablespoons chopped parsley
- ¼ teaspoon nutmeg
- Salt & pepper to taste
- 1 lb fresh pasta sheets, 6 x 8 inches
- ⅔ cup grated asiago, reggiano or parmesan cheese
- ¼ cup bread crumbs

Toast pine nuts in a heavy-bottomed sauté pan until golden brown, chop finely and set aside.

Sauté onion in oil until tender. Add garlic and spinach and sauté until heated through. Add wine and cook until liquid evaporates. Let cool.

In a separate bowl mix together bread crumbs, ricotta cheese, egg, and seasoning. Add spinach and toasted pine nuts; mix well.

Pre-cook pasta in boiling salted water one sheet at a time for 30 seconds each. Remove with a strainer and place in ice water briefly to cool. Place separately on a towel to dry.

Preheat oven to 375 °F

Butter a 9 x 13 inch baking dish. Ladle enough sauce into the pan to cover the entire surface, about ⅓ cup.

Working one sheet at a time, moisten pasta with a little oil or water. Spread filling thinly over the pasta to within ½ inch of the edge. Roll into a cylinder and place seam side down in baking dish. Repeat until all the filling has been used. Top with remaining sauce, breadcrumbs and grated cheese. Bake until golden brown, approximately 25 minutes.

Baked Cannelloni, pictured here without the sauce.

I love the *time and in between*
the *calm inside* me
in the space where *I can breathe*
I believe there is a distance I have wandered to touch
upon the years of *reaching out*
reaching in holding out *holding in...*

Roasted Root Vegetable Stew

serves 6–8

Preheat oven to 350°F

- 12 pearl onions, peeled
- 1 sweet potato, peeled and cut
  into bite-sized chunks
- 1 white potato, peeled and cut
  into bite-sized chunks
- 6 baby purple russet potatoes, peeled,
  or 6 new potatoes
- 2 parsnips, peeled and diced
- 1 large carrot, peeled and diced
- 2 beets, diced
- 12 asparagus stalks
- 1 cup button mushrooms
- ¼ cup canola oil
- 1 bunch thyme, chopped

Cook the onions, potatoes, parsnips, carrots
and beets separately in boiling water
until slightly tender, making sure to cook
the beets last.

Blanch the asparagus, cut into thirds and
place on a baking sheet with the mushrooms
and parboiled vegetables. Toss with canola
oil and thyme and bake until the vegetables
begin to caramelize, about 15–20 minutes.

Miso Gravy

- 1 cup red wine
- 3 tablespoons red miso paste
- 3 cups vegetable stock
- 2 tablespoons cornstarch
- 2 tablespoons cold water

Bring the red wine to a boil. Reduce heat
and add miso paste and vegetable stock. Mix
the cornstarch and water together and
add to the gravy. Cook and stir until thick
and bubbly. Toss the ingredients together
and serve.

Portobello mushrooms are the fully mature version of the common mushrooms we're used to eating. Their meaty texture and full flavour makes them a great addition to salads, sandwiches and pastas, where they'll often be grilled and sliced. This recipe calls for whole portobellos, creating a presentation that is as dramatic as the dish is flavourful.

Portobello Mushroom Stack

serves 4

- 2 pints vine-ripened cherry tomatoes
- Assorted chopped herbs, such as rosemary and thyme
- 5 basil leaves, shredded
- Olive oil
- 8 Portobello mushrooms, stems removed
- 6 eggs, lightly beaten
- 2 sprigs of rosemary, finely chopped
- 1 sprig of thyme, finely chopped
- 1/4 cup parmesan cheese
- Salt & pepper to taste
- 3 cups bread crumbs (Japanese if available) or matzo meal
- 1/2 cup canola oil for sauté
- 4 garlic cloves, chopped
- 2 cups cooked spinach
- 3 roma tomatoes, sliced
- 2 cups grated mozzarella cheese
- Grated parmesan for garnish

Preheat oven to 350°F

Cut the cherry tomatoes in half and place cut side down on a lightly oiled baking sheet. Sprinkle with chopped herbs and shredded basil. Brush with olive oil and bake until the tops begin to brown and the tomatoes have wilted. Season with salt and pepper and set aside.

Meanwhile, carefully remove the mushroom stems and discard. Mix eggs, herbs, parmesan cheese, and seasoning together. Dip one mushroom at a time into the egg mixture, then into the bread crumbs, coating evenly. Panfry the mushrooms in canola oil until golden brown on both sides. Drain on a paper towel.

Sauté garlic; add spinach, salt and pepper and sauté until the spinach wilts. If using frozen spinach thaw first and drain out excess water before cooking.

To assemble
Place panfried mushrooms on a baking sheet. Top with sliced tomatoes and grated mozzarella and bake until the cheese melts.

Remove the mushrooms from the oven and place the sautéed spinach on top of four of the mushrooms. Place a cheese-topped mushroom on top of the spinach.

To serve, place a mushroom stack in the centre of a plate. Garnish with wilted tomatoes and grated parmesan. To add colour, substitute yellow baby tomatoes for half the cherry tomatoes before wilting.

Portobello Mushrooms

I was first introduced to Thai food when I went to Thailand for World Vision. I fell in love with the rich, exotic flavours of their food. Jaime's version of Thai Whitefish Curry brings back many memories of a very special trip.

This curry calls for a few esoteric ingredients, which can be found in most Asian markets. Galangal, widely used in Thai cooking, is a member of the ginger family. Sometimes it's sold in powdered form under the name "Laos powder."

Thai Whitefish Curry

serves 6–8

- 3 small onions, finely chopped
- 3 tablespoons vegetable oil
- 2 cloves garlic, crushed
- 3 tablespoons grated ginger
- 1 stick lemon grass (use tender part and finely chop)
- 1 tablespoon red curry paste (or to taste)
- ½ cup sweet Thai chili sauce
- ½ cup fish sauce
- 4 cups coconut milk
- 8 kaffir lime leaves
- 2 small pieces dried galangal or 1 teaspoon galangal powder
- 2 lbs orange roughy or other whitefish cut into 1 inch pieces
- 12 medium scallops
- 8 medium shrimp, peeled and deveined
- 1 cup chopped cilantro
- 8 Thai basil leaves

Sauté onions in oil until translucent. Add garlic and ginger and cook for 1 minute. Add lemon grass, curry paste, chili and fish sauce and cook for 2 minutes. Add coconut milk, lime leaves, and galangal. Cook over low heat for about 15 minutes. Add fish, scallops and shrimp, bring to a boil, and cook for 10 minutes or until the fish is done. Add the cilantro and basil. If using dried galangal, remove before serving.

Sometimes we'll have friends over for dinner on a moment's notice. This dish, which is super easy to prepare, is great served with a loaf of French bread and a tossed salad.

This pesto is also great on pasta or fish. It's easy to make in a food processor, but if you don't have one just chop the ingredients up as finely as possible. A blender is not recommended because there's not enough liquid for the blender to work properly.

Sundried Tomato and Pecan Pesto with Prawns

serves 4

- 2 small cloves garlic
- ¼ cup pecans
- 1–2 tablespoons olive oil
- 2 heaping tablespoons oil-packed
  sundried tomatoes
- 2 heaping tablespoons parmesan cheese
- ½ cup basil leaves (spinach will do
  in a pinch)
- 1 lb prawns, shelled and deveined
- 2 tablespoons butter or oil

Combine garlic, pecans, oil, sundried tomatoes, cheese and basil together in a food processor and process until smooth.

Over medium heat, sauté prawns in butter or oil until they turn pink all over, about 5–7 minutes. Toss with pesto and serve.

Tiger Prawns with Soba Noodles

serves 4

Tiger Prawns

- 1¼ lbs tiger prawns (21–25 count)
- 1½ tablespoons rice vinegar
- 1 tablespoon lime juice
- ½ teaspoon fish sauce
- ¼ teaspoon dark sesame oil
- 2 teaspoons five-spice powder
- 1 teaspoon Tabasco
- 1½ teaspoons minced ginger root
- 2 cloves garlic, minced

Peel and devein the prawns under cold running water. Combine remaining ingredients, add prawns and marinate for at least an hour.

Cook prawns on a hot grill for about 3 minutes on each side. Reserve marinade to toss with soba noodles.

Soba Noodles

- 1 lb fresh soba noodles
- Canola or peanut oil for frying
- Reserved marinade

Cook soba noodles according to package directions. Drain well. Stir-fry the noodles for about 2 minutes, add remaining marinade and toss gently. Serve with grilled prawns.

We had a lot of fun with this presentation, using a wooden skewer to stack soba noodles and prawns on top of each other.

It's important to remember that cooking should be fun—never be afraid to experiment with ingredients or presentation. All it takes is a little imagination to make a dish spectacular.

Louisiana Crab Cakes

serves 4

- ½ cup mayonnaise
- 3 eggs, slightly beaten
- 2 teaspoons hot mustard
- 1¼ lbs lump crab meat, picked over
- 2 tablespoons chopped cilantro
- 2 tablespoons chopped red pepper
- 2 tablespoons sliced green onion
- 1 teaspoon pickled relish
- 2 cups breadcrumbs
- 1 teaspoon Old Bay seasoning (optional)
- 1 teaspoon cayenne pepper or hot sauce
- Breadcrumbs for coating

Stir the mayonnaise, eggs and mustard together. Fold in the crab meat. Add cilantro, red pepper, green onion and relish. Gently fold in the bread crumbs, bay seasoning and cayenne. Form small cakes and coat with bread crumbs. Panfry gently in butter until golden brown.

Peppers

The combination of salsa and fish is both refreshing and satisfying. Before cooking, the fish is coated with a spicy paste and seared, creating a delicious crispy skin.

Chilean Sea Bass with Spicy Fruit Salsa

serves 4–6

Spicy Fruit Salsa

- 1 teaspoon chopped jalapeño or
  other hot pepper
- 1 small red onion, finely chopped
- 1 papaya, peeled, seeded and chopped
- 1 ripe mango, peeled, pitted and diced
- ½ cup fresh pineapple, peeled and chopped
- ½ lemon, juiced
- ½ lime, juiced
- 1 tablespoon honey
- ½ teaspoon chili powder
- 1 tablespoon chopped cilantro
- ¼ cup olive or vegetable oil
- Pinch of salt and pepper

Wearing rubber gloves, remove jalapeño seeds and membrane and discard. Prepare all the above ingredients, combine, and refrigerate.

Spicy Paste

- ¼ cup olive oil
- 1 tablespoon chili powder
- 1 tablespoon ground cumin
- ½ tablespoon curry powder
- ¼ teaspoon turmeric
- ¼ teaspoon paprika
- ¼ teaspoon garlic powder
- ¼ teaspoon onion powder
- ½ teaspoon anise seed
- ½ teaspoon mustard seed, toasted
  in a dry sauté pan for 1 minute.

Combine the above ingredients together to form a spicy paste.

Sea Bass

- 4 Chilean sea bass filets (or whitefish
  of your choice)
- Salt and pepper
- ¼ cup flour for coating
- Vegetable or canola oil for sauté

Preheat oven to 375°F

Season fish with salt and pepper and coat with flour. Brush a heavy coating of the spice mixture on the skin of the fish. Add 2 tablespoons of oil to a very hot oven-safe skillet and sear the fish skin side down. When the skin is crispy, place the fish in the oven for approximately 10–12 minutes until done. Serve with spicy fruit salsa.

This spectacular presentation was created by placing the fish filet in a vertical position on the plate. A serving of spicy fruit salsa and a garnish of star fruit, papaya, and pineapple leaf finishes off the elegant look. We served it on a bed of crispy fried potatoes.

When I was a child the most exotic tuna dish I tasted was tuna casserole. When Jaime prepares tuna I almost can't believe it's the same fish. The melt in your mouth texture and full rich flavour make these two dishes very popular.

This dish requires that sushi grade tuna be used, which is usually bought frozen from Japanese markets or specialty fish stores. If you're unsure about the grade of tuna, be sure to ask. Keep the fish refrigerated while preparing the other ingredients.

Japanese-Style Tuna Tartare
serves 4

- ¼ cup cucumber, peeled, seeded and very finely chopped
- ¼ cup finely chopped red pepper
- 1 tablespoon finely chopped ginger
- 2 tablespoons finely chopped green onion
- 2 garlic cloves, pulverized
- 3 tablespoons wasabi paste (Japanese horseradish)
- ½ cup soy sauce
- 1 tablespoon mirin (Japanese rice wine)
- 1 tablespoon black and white sesame seeds, toasted
- A pinch of chili paste
- Hot bean paste to taste (optional)
- A splash of sesame oil
- 1 lb very high quality sushi grade tuna, finely chopped

Make sure your work surface and knives are very clean before beginning. Place a serving bowl in the fridge to chill. Prepare all the ingredients, except the tuna, and mix together. Refrigerate.

Chop the tuna very finely and place in the refrigerated serving bowl. Add the other prepared ingredients and refrigerate until serving.

This salsa was inspired by the classic Salade Niçoise.

Grilled Tuna with Niçoise Salsa

serves 4

Marinade

- ¼ cup chopped onion
- 2 cloves garlic, chopped
- ½ cup olive oil
- 1 tablespoon Dijon mustard
- 1 teaspoon dry mustard
- 1 tablespoon lemon pepper (or chopped lemon zest with black pepper)
- 1 tablespoon chopped tarragon
- 1 tablespoon honey
- ¼ cup soy sauce
- 4 very fresh tuna steaks, trimmed

Combine all the ingredients, except tuna, together in a bowl. Mix well. Add tuna and marinate for at least 1 hour.

Salsa

- ¼ lb fresh green beans, ends removed, cooked and chopped
- ¼ lb fresh yellow beans, ends removed, cooked and chopped
- 1 small red onion, chopped
- 1 small white onion, chopped
- 2 large tomatoes, seeded and chopped
- 1 yellow tomato, seeded and chopped (optional)
- 1 cucumber, peeled, seeded and finely chopped
- ¼ cup chopped black olives
- 2 tablespoons capers, drained and washed
- ½ cup canned white beans, drained and rinsed
- 6 oil-packed anchovy filets, rinsed and chopped
- ¼ cup olive oil
- ½ lemon, juiced
- 3 tablespoons red wine vinegar
- 4 tablespoons chopped fresh chives
- Salt and pepper to taste
- 2 hard-boiled eggs (or 4 hard-boiled quail eggs), shelled and halved, for garnish

Steam or parboil the green and yellow beans and rinse in cold water. Combine all the ingredients, except the hard boiled eggs, together in a bowl and refrigerate.

Grill the marinated tuna for about 4 minutes on each side. Tuna is best served medium rare, so be careful not to over cook it. To serve, simply top grilled tuna with salsa. Garnish with hard boiled eggs. Pass extra salsa at the table.

Galangal

Ginger

Here's a simple teriyaki salmon that's great served with sautéed bok choy. Sticky rice coated with black and white sesame seeds adds a bit of intrigue to the plate.

Black and White Salmon Teriyaki

serves 4

Marinade

- *1/3 cup sake*
- *1/2 cup mirin (Japanese rice wine)*
- *1/2 cup soy sauce*
- *1 tablespoon honey*
- *1 tablespoon grated ginger*
- *4 pieces of salmon*

Mix the marinade ingredients together. Add the fish and marinate for at least an hour, turning once.

Preheat oven to 475°F

Line a baking sheet with foil and spray with cooking spray. Remove fish from marinade, reserving marinade for basting. Place fish on the baking sheet skin side down.

Turn the preheated oven to broil. Place fish on the top rack and broil for about 10 minutes, basting once or twice until the skin becomes crispy. Baste the fish again, cover with foil and turn the oven back to 475°F. Cook for 6–8 minutes until done. Meanwhile, cook the bok choy.

Bok choy

- *1 teaspoon ground ginger*
- *1 clove crushed garlic*
- *1 tablespoon sesame oil*
- *2 cups bok choy*
- *1 tablespoon soy sauce*

Sauté ginger and garlic in sesame oil. Add bok choy and sauté until fork tender. Season with soy sauce.

Rice Balls

- *1 cup sushi rice (or any short grain sticky rice)*
- *Black and white sesame seeds (optional)*

Cook the rice according to package directions. When done, cool slightly and form into balls. Roll each rice ball in the sesame seeds.

This dish is great served with crispy wontons, which are simply julienned wonton wrappers deep-fried in hot vegetable oil until golden.

The Salmon Teriyaki, pictured here with crispy wontons, is garnished with baby bok choy.

This spectacular dish is great for celebrations.
Serve with lots of great wine and loads of toasted garlic croutons.

Zuppa di Pesce Italian Fish Stew

serves 6

- ½ lb mussels
- ½ lb clams
- 6 large shrimp, peeled and deveined
- ½ lb squid
- 6 large bay scallops
- 3 lbs assorted fish (sea bass, monkfish, red mullet, mackerel, sole)
- 1½ cups white wine
- 1 cup clam broth
- 5 cups water
- 3 boiling potatoes, peeled and diced
- Fish heads and bones (optional)
- 1 large onion, chopped
- 4 cloves garlic, chopped
- ½ teaspoon chili flakes
- ¼ cup olive oil
- Flour for dusting
- Salt and pepper
- 2 lbs or 10 roma tomatoes, diced
- ½ teaspoon saffron
- ¼ cup chopped parsley

Gently scrub mussels and remove beards if necessary. Tap any open mussels lightly on the counter and discard ones that don't shut instantly. Rinse the clams and give them the same shell test as the mussels. Peel and devein the shrimp. Clean the squid by removing the cartilage and rinsing. Cut into circles. Cut the assorted fish into slightly larger than bite-size pieces.

Heat the white wine, clam broth, and 5 cups of water with the diced potatoes (fish heads and bones can be added for flavour) and reduce by one-half. Bring to a boil and cook until the potatoes are tender.

In a large pot sauté onion, garlic and chili flakes in oil. Season fish with salt and pepper, dredge in flour and place skin side down in the hot oil. When the fish is slightly browned, ladle in reduced stock and cooked potatoes. Add squid and tomatoes. Finally, add the mussels, scallops, clams, shrimp and saffron and cook covered for an additional 5 minutes, or until shellfish open. Discard any shellfish that do not open. Garnish with parsley and serve.

Steamed Black Mussels

serves 2

- 30 black mussels
- 1 cup white wine
- 1 cup clam broth
- ¼ cup olive oil
- ¼ cup finely chopped onion
- 4 cloves garlic, chopped
- ½ cup lemon pieces
- ½ cup chopped fresh tomato
- 3 tablespoons chopped parsley
- 1 tablespoon butter
- Salt & pepper to taste
- Toast points (optional)
- Olive oil

Gently scrub mussels and remove beards if necessary. Tap any open mussels lightly on the counter and discard any that don't shut instantly.

Bring white wine and clam broth to a boil. Reduce heat and simmer for 10 minutes.

In a large pot sauté the onions and garlic in oil, being careful not to brown the garlic. Add the cleaned mussels and hot broth. Cover and steam over moderately high heat for 4–7 minutes, or until the mussels have opened. Discard any unopened mussels.

Uncover, add the lemon, tomato, parsley, butter, salt and pepper and cook another minute. Place mussels in a large bowl and garnish with toast points and a drizzle of olive oil.

Toast Points
- 1 loaf crusty Italian bread
- 1 or 2 cloves garlic, whole, peeled

Slice the bread and lightly toast it. When cooled, gently rub with garlic.

I grew up on the east coast, so I love lobster. Now it's sort of a tradition for Jaime to serve lobster just once on tour, at the very end, when we're all saying good-bye to everyone we've worked so closely with for so many months.

This recipe uses a flavoured butter that's rolled into a cylinder shape. It can be sliced into round pats for broiling or barbecuing and stored in the fridge for later use. While this recipe calls for live lobster, frozen will do just as well.

Sweet Surrender
Lobster with Candied Ginger and Mango Herb Butter

serves 4–6

Mango Herb Butter
- ½ pound unsalted butter, softened
- 2 tablespoons finely chopped chervil
- 2 tablespoons finely chopped parsley
- 2 tablespoons finely chopped mango
- 1 tablespoon finely chopped candied ginger
- 1 teaspoon sugar or honey

Mix the butter with the chervil, parsley, mango, ginger and honey until it forms a paste. Transfer the mixture to the centre of a sheet of plastic wrap and roll into a 5 inch long cylinder. Chill until firm.

Boiled Lobster
- 1 large onion, sliced
- A few crushed black peppercorns
- 1 bay leaf
- Salt to taste
- 4 medium sized lobsters (or 4 to 6 cups cooked lobster meat)

Place the onions, peppercorns and bay leaf in a large pot of boiling, salty water. Plunge the lobsters headfirst into the pot.

Return to a boil, reduce heat and simmer for 6–8 minutes per pound. Remove the lobster and run it under cool water. Remove the meat by splitting the body cavity and claws in half with scissors.

Arrange lobster meat in a broiler-safe dish; add salt and pepper to taste. Cut six ¼ inch slices off the butter cylinder and place on top of the lobster. Broil until the butter is melted and lobster is heated through.

If serving whole boiled lobster, simply melt the mango herb butter and serve as a dip.

Lobster tails served with a mango herb butter disc and toast points, garnished with a pink oyster mushroom.

Desserts and Beverages

This is a simple dessert with a sophisticated flavour.

Baked Peaches

serves 8

Preheat oven to 350°F

- 4 large yellow peaches
- 1½ cups crushed macaroons
  or amaretto cookies
- 2–3 tablespoons almond liqueur
  (such as amaretto)
- 6 tablespoons sugar
- ½ cup crushed almonds
- 3 tablespoons butter, melted
- 1½ cups white wine

Cut peaches in half and remove pits. Scoop about ¼ of the insides out of each half and mix with the crushed macaroons, liqueur, sugar, almonds and melted butter. Stuff the centre of each peach and place in a shallow baking dish. Pour white wine over the peaches and bake for 20–25 minutes.

When trying to write songs after experiencing writer's block, one sure-fire remedy is baking cookies. It's easy and they always turn out great. I can't say it makes the songs come any easier, but it does cheer me up!

Writer's Block Oatmeal-Raisin Cookies

makes 2 dozen large cookies

Preheat oven to 350°F

- 1 cup butter, softened
- 1½ cups dark brown sugar
- 2 eggs
- 2 teaspoons vanilla
- 2 teaspoons water
- 2 cups flour
- 1 teaspoon baking soda
- 1 teaspoon baking powder
- ½ teaspoon salt
- 2 teaspoons cinnamon
- ¼ teaspoon ground cloves
- ½ teaspoon allspice
- 2 cups rolled oats
- 1–2 cups raisins

Cream butter until light and fluffy. Gradually add sugar. Add eggs, vanilla and water and beat until smooth.

Sift dry ingredients together. Add to the butter mixture and mix well. Fold in oats and raisins.

Drop by spoonfuls onto a greased cookie sheet, leaving enough space for the cookies to spread out. Bake 8–10 minutes, until golden.

Jaime's sister Fran makes a wicked chocolate chip cookie. We coaxed her into sharing the recipe with us.

Fran's Famous Chocolate Chip Cookies

makes 3 dozen big ones

Preheat oven to 350°F

- 1 lb butter, softened
- 1½ cups white sugar
- 1½ cups light brown sugar
- 4 eggs
- 2½ teaspoons vanilla extract
- 5½ cups all-purpose flour, sifted
- 2 teaspoons salt
- 2 teaspoons baking soda
- 4–5 cups chocolate chips
- 2 cups chopped pecans
- 1 cup shredded coconut

Cream the butter until light and fluffy. Gradually add the sugar, continuing to cream until all the sugar is used. Add eggs, one at a time, beating well after each addition. Stir in the vanilla.

Sift together the flour, salt and baking soda. Add all at once to the butter mixture, stirring well with a wooden spoon. Add chocolate chips, pecans and coconut and stir until mixed.

Form dough into large balls and press down lightly on an ungreased non-stick baking sheet. Bake until golden, about 15 minutes, being careful not to brown the edges. Remove from oven and place baking sheet on a wire rack; cool 5 minutes. Transfer cookies to rack; cool completely.

Hint: Take half the cookie dough, put it in a ziplock bag and freeze it for a rainy day.

This dish is made upside down and then flipped over to serve. Arrange the apples the way you want to see them when the tart is inverted out of the pan. The dish starts on top of the stove and finishes in the oven, so you'll need an oven-friendly sauté pan. When done the apples will have a beautiful caramel colour. Apple tart is great served warm with vanilla ice cream and a dusting of powdered sugar.

Grandma's Upside-Down Apple Tart

serves 4–6

- A handful of all-purpose flour
- 1 sheet frozen puff pastry dough, thawed
- 6 Granny Smith apples, peeled, cored and sliced into thin wedges
- Juice of 1/2 lemon
- 1 teaspoon vanilla extract
- 1 teaspoon cinnamon
- 1/4 cup butter
- 3/4 cup sugar

Preheat oven to 375°F

Dust a work surface with flour. Roll pastry dough into a 1/8 inch thick circle, starting from the centre of the dough and working towards the edge. Place a 12 inch sauté pan upside down on the dough and trace around it with a small knife. The resulting circle will fit perfectly in the pan. Refrigerate until needed.

Peel, core and slice the apples. Gently toss with lemon juice, vanilla and cinnamon.

Melt butter and sugar over high heat in an oven-friendly sauté pan until golden brown. Reduce heat and place the apples in layers of concentric circles in the pan, being careful not to let the sugar burn. The mixture will bubble around the sides of the apples and should have the colour and consistency of maple syrup.

When the apples begin to soften, cover with the pastry circle. Poke a few holes to let the steam escape. Cook for 3 minutes, place the pan in the oven, and bake for 10 minutes or until golden brown.

Remove from the oven and let rest for 2 minutes. Using oven mitts, place an inverted platter on top of the sauté pan and in one fast motion flip it so that the apples face up. Serve warm.

Blueberry-Almond Crisp

serves 4–6

Preheat oven to 375°F

- 1 cup almonds, toasted
- 15 sheets phyllo pastry
- 1/2 cup butter, melted
- 1/2 cup brown sugar
- 2 tablespoons cinnamon
- 8 graham crackers, crushed fine
- 2 pints blueberries, fresh or frozen

Place almonds on a cookie sheet and toast in the oven until golden. Crush with a rolling pin.

Mix the brown sugar and cinnamon together. Brush a phyllo sheet with butter, sprinkle with sugar and almonds. Place another layer on top and repeat. Repeat a third time and place the layers in a shallow, buttered 9 inch round baking dish. Continue working with phyllo, three at a time, until all phyllo has been used up.

Sprinkle graham crumbs over the phyllo and add the blueberries. Bake until golden brown, about 15 minutes. Serve warm with vanilla ice cream.

My Favourite Strawberry-Rhubarb Pie

serves 8

Pie Dough

This makes one 9 inch pie shell. You'll need
a pastry top and bottom, so either double
this recipe and make the pie top at the same
time, or make the top and bottom separately.

- 1 1/4 cups flour
- 1/2 teaspoon salt
- 1/2 cup butter or shortening, chilled
- 2-3 tablespoons water

Sift together flour and salt. Cut butter into
chunks and work into the flour until pea-
sized lumps form. Add 2-3 tablespoons cold
water and work as little as possible, in
order to avoid a stiff dough. As soon as the
dough sticks together, stop.

Form into a ball and roll out on a flat,
dry, lightly floured surface or on a piece
of cheesecloth lightly dusted with flour.
Roll out until slightly larger than a
9 inch pie plate.

Preheat oven to 400°F

Filling

- 2 cups sliced rhubarb
- 2 cups halved strawberries
- 1/2 cup sugar
- 1-2 teaspoons grated orange peel
- 3 tablespoons flour
- 1/8 teaspoon salt
- 2 tablespoons butter

Cut rhubarb into 1 inch slices. Cut
strawberries in half. Combine with sugar,
orange peel, flour and salt and mix
gently. Pour into an unbaked pie shell
and place small dollops of butter all
over the top. Place a layer of pastry on
top, pressing the top and bottom layers
together to create a seal. Flute the edges
any way you like, making sure the
mixture is sealed in, or it will bubble all
over the oven and make a real mess.
Score the top of the pastry with a small,
sharp knife, cutting in any design you
like. Bake for about 40-45 minutes, until
the crust is golden brown.

97

Jaime often jokes that I'm addicted to mangoes. After trying this dessert you'll probably understand why.

This recipe is simple and easy to make on a moment's notice. For a low-fat version, simply use vegetable spray in place of butter; it works just as well.

Mango and Cherry Strudel
2 strudels

- *1 cup dried cherries or cranberries*
- *1/4 cup peach or apricot brandy*
- *3 very ripe mangoes, peeled, pitted and finely chopped*
- *1/2 cup finely chopped almonds*
- *1/4 cup orange blossom or regular honey*
- *1/2 cup light brown sugar*
- *1 teaspoon vanilla*
- *Juice of 1 lemon*
- *Zest of 1 lemon*
- *1/4 teaspoon allspice*
- *1/4 teaspoon cinnamon*
- *1 package phyllo*
- *1/4 cup butter, melted, or vegetable spray*

Preheat oven to 350˚F

Mix the cherries and brandy together and let sit for 15 minutes. Drain. Mix the mangoes, almonds, honey, sugar, vanilla, lemon juice, lemon zest, allspice and cinnamon together with the cherries.

Lay a sheet of phyllo dough on top of a piece of waxed paper. Brush with melted butter, or spray with vegetable spray. Place another sheet on top and butter or spray, repeating the procedure six times.

Place the mango mixture on the dough, gently spreading it across the pastry. To avoid a wet strudel, gently wring the mixture out with your hands before placing it on the dough.

Roll the strudel up and tuck in the ends. Place seam side down on greased baking sheet. Score the top of the pastry with a sharp knife. Brush lightly with butter or spray; bake for 25 minutes or until golden brown.

Variation: Try adding a few pieces of chopped, candied ginger to the mango mixture.

Mango and Cherry Strudel served on mango purée and garnished with edible flowers.

The road stretches *like a memory* waiting to be revealed.
We pass through so *many stories* and so *many lives* every day.

There's *so much* to take in that
it's usually not until *the tour is over* that
there's *time to reflect* on all we've been through
and all *we've seen.*

This delicious low-fat dessert looks spectacular when finished. It consists of tuiles, which are thin, round cookies or wafers, layered with mango-blueberry cream. Parchment paper, which is available at most grocery stores in the plastic wrap section, is used to create a stencil for the tuiles.

Mango-Blueberry Napoleon

serves 4

Preheat oven to 400°F

Makes about 12 tuiles
- 2 egg whites
- 1/2 cup powdered sugar
- 1/4 cup oats
- 2 tablespoons wheat germ
- 1/4 cup all-purpose flour
- 1/4 teaspoon ground ginger
- 2 tablespoons butter, melted
- 1/4 teaspoon vanilla extract
- Parchment paper

Whip the egg whites until frothy. Gradually add the powdered sugar. Stir in oats, wheat germ, flour, and ginger.

Mix the melted butter and vanilla extract together and stream into the egg white mixture. Refrigerate for 30 minutes.

Place a piece of parchment paper on a cookie sheet. Using a drinking glass, trace circles with a pencil, leaving 1/2 inch between each circle. Use two sheets if necessary. Flip the parchment over and tack down each corner with a bit of tuile dough to keep parchment from curling up while baking. Grease with butter.

Place about 2 teaspoons of the tuile dough in the centre of each circle, spreading the dough out evenly. Bake for about 5 minutes, until golden brown. Remove from paper and set aside. Each dessert requires 3 tuiles.

For the Mango-Blueberry Cream
- 1 cup non-fat cream cheese
- 1/2 cup non-fat sour cream
- 2 tablespoons granulated sugar
- 1 orange, zested and squeezed
- 1 mango, peeled, pitted, and diced
- 1 pint blueberries, de-stemmed

Mix cream cheese and sour cream together on low speed until smooth. Add the sugar and mix on medium speed, scraping the sides of the bowl. Add the zest and orange juice. Fold in diced mango and blueberries.

To Assemble
Place a tuile in the centre of a plate. Put a dollop of mango-blueberry cream on top; place another tuile on top followed by more cream. Alternate until there are three layers. Garnish with a mint sprig.

For an added touch puree a peeled mango until smooth, add 1/4 cup orange juice and serve as a sauce with the Napoleon.

I like to make this dessert when we have friends over for dinner. It's simple and quick and satisfies my sweet tooth.

Baked Caramel Custard

serves 6

Preheat oven to 350°F

- *½ cup brown sugar*
- *2 cups skim milk*
- *¼ cup sugar*
- *⅛ teaspoon salt*
- *3 eggs, beaten*
- *½ teaspoon vanilla extract*

Melt brown sugar in a saucepan over medium heat until it turns to liquid and begins to caramelize. Pour into 6 custard cups, shaking cups to make sure the sugar is evenly distributed. Don't touch the sugar because it will be very hot.

Mix the remaining ingredients together and pour into each custard cup. Fill a large baking pan with 1 inch of hot water. Place custard cups in the water bath and bake for about 50–60 minutes. Remove from the oven and cool in the baking pan until they reach room temperature. Remove from water bath and chill.

To serve, quickly turn each cup over either onto individual serving plates or onto a large serving tray. The sugar will have turned into a delicious syrupy glaze. For an extra treat, serve with fruit and whipped cream.

Caramel Custard garnished with whipped cream and fruit. For a spectacular presentation Jaime caramelized some sugar and created a ship by drizzling the hot sugar onto greased wax paper.

It's the *simple things* in life that I enjoy the most—
reconnecting with *friends and family* for dinner
is a great way to enter into the orbit of home and
sanctuary after a long road trip.

This recipe uses candied ginger, which is readily available at most gourmet stores and Asian markets.

Full of Grace Soufflé

1 serving

- 1 tablespoon prepared instant
  vanilla pudding
- ½ teaspoon lemon zest
- ½ teaspoon orange zest
- ½ teaspoon finely chopped candied ginger
- 1 teaspoon lemon juice
- 2 egg whites
- Butter
- Sugar

Preheat oven to 400°F

Combine pudding with lemon zest, orange
zest, candied ginger and lemon juice.

Beat the egg whites to a stiff peak. Gently
fold into the pudding, half at a time.

Brush a soufflé mold with butter, and sugar
the sides. Fill to the brim and level off
with a butter knife. Fill a 9 x 13 inch baking
dish with ½ inch of hot water. Place soufflé
in the water. Bake until soufflé rises and
is golden brown, about 25–30 minutes. Don't
open the oven door while it's cooking or
it will fall.

Just before serving, this rich, chilled custard is sprinkled with brown sugar and broiled. The sugar becomes brittle, creating a delicious flavour as well as a textural contrast to the smooth, creamy custard. Crème Brûlée is usually baked in small porcelain or ceramic baking dishes called ramekins.

Crème Brûlée

serves 8

- *4 cups heavy cream*
- *One vanilla bean, split lengthwise in half or 2 teaspoons vanilla extract*
- *1 cup white sugar*
- *8 egg yolks*
- *1 whole egg*
- *Raw sugar as needed*

Preheat oven to 325°F

Bring cream, vanilla bean and half the sugar to a boil.

In a separate bowl, mix together the rest of the sugar, yolks and whole egg. Slowly mix about one third of the hot cream into the egg mixture. When blended, add the egg mixture back into the hot cream.

Strain the mixture and pour into small ramekins. Fill a 9 x 13 inch baking dish with ½ inch of hot water. Place ramekins in the water and bake for about 30 minutes.

Remove from the oven and cool at room temperature for about 30 minutes, keeping the ramekins in the water. Once the ramekins are cool, remove from the water and store in the fridge until ready to serve.

Just before serving sprinkle 1 tablespoon of sugar over each ramekin. Fill a 9 x 13 inch baking dish with ½ inch of ice water. and broil until the sugar forms a hard crust.

Crème Brûlée served with a nest of caramelized sugar. Jaime created the nested look by drizzling caramelized sugar over a greased inverted bowl. He then waited until it cooled, gently removed it, and placed it on top of the ramekin after broiling.

Laughter is the best cure for anything that ails you.

Whenever there's a birthday on the road, we always have a cake to celebrate—sometimes things get a little out of hand...

This cake is perfect for any celebration. It uses beet juice, which gives it a very festive look.

Love Cake

serves 10

Preheat oven to 350°F

- 1 cup vegetable shortening
- 1½ cups sugar
- 2 eggs
- 2 tablespoons cocoa powder
- ¼ cup beet juice
- a few drops red food colouring (optional)
- ½ teaspoon salt
- 1 teaspoon vanilla
- 1 cup buttermilk
- 2¼ cups flour (sifted three times)
- 1 tablespoon vinegar
- 1 teaspoon baking soda

Grease two 9 inch round cake tins.

Cream shortening and sugar together until light and fluffy. Add eggs and beat 1 minute. In a separate bowl, mix cocoa powder, beet juice, food colouring and salt together to form a paste. Add to the shortening mixture and stir until well blended. Mix vanilla and buttermilk together and add alternately to the shortening mixture with the flour, about a third at a time.

Mix vinegar and baking soda together in a cup and add to the batter. Gently stir just until blended. Bake for 30 minutes. Cool cake in pans for 10 minutes; remove from pans and continue cooling on racks.

Icing
- 1 cup milk
- 7 tablespoons flour
- 1 cup butter, softened
- 1 cup icing sugar, sifted
- 1 teaspoon vanilla

Mix milk and flour together and cook over medium heat until thick. Refrigerate until completely cool.

Beat butter until light and fluffy. Gradually add sugar. Stir in vanilla. Add cooled milk mixture a little at a time and blend.

Phyllo makes an interesting serving dish for this light lemon dessert. Phyllo cups and filling can be prepared a day ahead.
Spoon mixture into cups right before serving.

Lemon Phyllo Cups

serves 12

Lemon Filling

- ½ cup sugar
- 2 tablespoons cornstarch
- ⅛ teaspoon salt
- 1 cup cold water
- ¼ cup fresh lemon juice
- 1 large egg, beaten
- ½ teaspoon grated lemon peel
- 1 teaspoon butter

Phyllo Cups

- Vegetable spray
- 4 sheets phyllo, thawed
- 2 tablespoons butter, melted
- 2 teaspoons sugar
- Assorted fruit
- Whipped cream

Preheat oven to 375°F

Combine sugar, cornstarch and salt together in a medium saucepan. Gradually whisk in water and lemon juice until sugar and cornstarch dissolve. Whisk in beaten egg and lemon peel and cook over medium heat, stirring often, until thick and bubbly, about 5 minutes. Remove from heat and stir in butter. Transfer to a bowl and press plastic wrap on the surface of the mixture. Allow to cool at room temperature.

For Phyllo Cups

Lightly spray twelve ⅓ cup muffin tins with vegetable spray. Stack 4 phyllo sheets on a flat work surface and cut into six 4-inch squares, forming a total of 24 squares. Press one phyllo square into each cup. Using a pastry brush, dab phyllo with melted butter. Press another phyllo square on top of the first, making sure the corners are at different angles. Lightly brush with butter; sprinkle with sugar.

Bake until golden brown, about 6 minutes. Cool on a wire rack for 10 minutes; remove from tins and continue cooling.

Spoon lemon filling into the phyllo cups. Place assorted fruit, such as kiwi, strawberries, blueberries or raspberries gently on top. Top with whipped cream.

We had some fun with this presentation, placing the phyllo in a teacup before filling it. We then garnished it with edible flowers and a caramelized sugar design, made by drizzling caramelized sugar onto greased wax paper.

"Smile"

These simple low-fat fruit tarts are easy to prepare.

Fruit Tart with Lemon Cream

12 tarts

Preheat oven to 400°F

Pastry

- 3 cups all-purpose flour
  2 teaspoons white sugar
- ½ teaspoon cinnamon
- Zest of 1 lemon
- ¼ cup chilled margarine
- 2 egg whites

Mix flour, sugar, cinnamon and lemon zest together in a bowl. Work chilled margarine into dry ingredients until small crumbs form. Add egg whites while gently stirring with a wooden spoon. Turn the dough out onto a lightly floured surface and knead until it forms a ball. Wrap with plastic and refrigerate for 30 minutes.

On a lightly floured surface roll the dough out to about ⅛ inch thick. Use a tin can or cookie cutter to cut out 12 circles. Place circles into muffin tins and gently form them to fit. Refrigerate for 10 minutes. Before baking, prick the dough with a fork. Bake until golden, about 15 minutes. Cool for 5 minutes. Remove from muffin tins and finish cooling on a wire rack. Set aside.

Lemon Cream

- 1½ cups low-fat yogurt
- 2 tablespoons sugar
- ½ teaspoon vanilla extract
- 2 tablespoons fresh lemon juice
- Zest of 1 lemon

Mix the yogurt, sugar, vanilla, lemon juice and lemon zest together and refrigerate.

To assemble

- 12 baked tart shells
- Lemon cream
- 12 small strawberries, halved
- 1 kiwi, cut into thin slices
- ½ mango, diced
- 36 blueberries
- 12 black grapes, sliced in half,
  or other assorted fruit of your choice

Spoon 2 tablespoons of lemon cream into each tart shell. Arrange the fruit on top of each tart.

Chocolate truffles can be served many different ways. Roll in powdered sugar, cocoa powder or crushed nuts, or add a small amount of your favourite liqueur. This recipe is simple, and the results are delicious.

Chocolate Truffles

makes about 2 dozen

- *¾ cup heavy cream*
- *2 cups chopped high quality semi-sweet chocolate, Ghirardelli or Lindt Swiss*

Heat cream in a small pot until it reaches a boil. Immediately remove from heat, pour over chocolate and cover with plastic wrap to allow the chocolate to melt.

Mix the cream and chocolate together until smooth and refrigerate until it reaches the consistency of fudge. When cool, use a spoon or melon baller to scoop out the chocolate. Roll into firm balls with your hands. Refrigerate.

To coat the truffles, melt a little bit of chocolate. Roll each truffle in the melted chocolate and then in the coating of your choice. Refrigerate.

Bittersweet Chocolate Truffle Cheesecake

serves 12

Preheat oven to 350°F

- 1 1/3 cups graham wafer crumbs
- 1/3 cup melted butter
- 1 lb cream cheese, softened
- 1 cup sugar
- 3 large eggs
- 1/4 cup cold espresso or strong coffee
- 8 ounces bittersweet chocolate, melted
- 1/2 cup sour cream

For the glaze
- 1/2 cup whipping cream
- 4 ounces bittersweet chocolate

Combine graham wafer crumbs and butter and press into the bottom and sides of a 9 inch spring-form pan. Refrigerate.

Beat cream cheese and sugar together until smooth. Add eggs one at a time, beating well after each addition. Add coffee and melted chocolate and mix well. Stir in sour cream.

Pour mixture into prepared pie crust and gently smooth out the top. Bake for 40–50 minutes or until the centre is barely set. Remove from the oven and cool completely on a wire rack. Before removing from the pan gently run a knife between the pan and the crust.

Bring the whipping cream to a simmer over low heat. Add the chocolate and stir until melted and smooth. Spoon over cake. For a garnish, shave some chocolate curls on top of the cake.

One of the most rewarding things in the world for me
is to *feel* the *love and admiration* of an *audience*
and the *connection we share* in the music—
it's such *a gift* and I'm very grateful for it.

Kahlua Tiramisu

serves 6–8

- *3/4 cup sugar*
- *4 eggs, separated*
- *2 tablespoons Kahlua*
- *2 1/2 cups heavy cream*
- *1 teaspoon vanilla, to taste*
- *1 teaspoon rum, to taste*
- *2 tablespoons Marsala wine*
- *4 egg whites*
- *4 tablespoons sugar*
- *1 cup mascarpone cheese or cream cheese*
- *1/4 cup espresso or coffee*
- *Ladyfingers, as needed*
- *Chocolate shavings*
  or mini chocolate chips, as needed
- *Cocoa powder, as needed*

Whip 3/4 cup sugar into the egg yolks until thick and pale yellow. Reduce speed to low and stream in the Kahlua. Set aside.

Whip cream until soft peaks form. Place 1/2 cup of cream in a bowl and gently fold in vanilla and rum. Set aside.

Fold the Marsala wine into the remaining whipped cream and reserve.

Whip the egg whites on high speed until frothy. Stream in the 4 tablespoons of sugar and whip on high for 1 minute. Reserve.

Gently mix mascarpone or cream cheese with the egg yolk mixture until just combined. Gently fold in the 1/2 cup whipped cream with a plastic spatula, using slow gentle motions. Slowly fold in the egg whites.

To assemble
Drizzle the coffee onto the ladyfingers. Place standing up in a parfait glass or bowl. Alternate layers of mascarpone mixture, marsala cream and chocolate shavings. Dust top with cocoa powder.

I definitely got my love of baking from my mom. I remember the wonderful smells that would come from the kitchen when she was baking cookies and pies—I just couldn't wait to dig in.

Banana Bread

I loaf

Preheat oven to 350°F

- ½ cup melted butter or light oil
- ¾ cup sugar
- 2 eggs, lightly beaten
- 2 large ripe bananas, mashed
- 1 teaspoon vanilla
- 1¼ cups flour
- 1 teaspoon baking soda
- 1 teaspoon baking powder
- ¼ cup chopped pecans (optional)

Combine the butter, sugar, eggs, bananas and vanilla. Set aside. In a separate bowl sift together flour, baking soda and baking powder. Add to the banana mixture and combine just until moist. Gently fold in the pecans. Pour into a greased loaf pan and bake for about 1 hour, or until a knife inserted in the centre comes out clean. Cool on a rack for 10 minutes; remove from pan and continue to cool on rack.

This currant cake recipe is actually my grandmother's. Many of the recipes I use today are ones I remember my mom making when I was little. Now when I go home at Christmas I constantly ask my mom how to make everything.

Mom's Currant Cake

1 loaf

Preheat oven to 325°F

- ½ cup cream or half and half
- 1 heaping tablespoon molasses
- ¾ cup butter
- ¾ cup Demerara sugar
- 3 eggs
- 2 cups currants
- 2⅔ cups flour
- 2 teaspoons baking powder
- ¼ teaspoon salt

Heat the cream and mix in molasses. In a separate bowl cream the butter until light and fluffy. Gradually add the sugar. Add the eggs, one at a time, beating well after each addition. Stir in the cream and molasses mixture, then add the currants.

Sift the dry ingredients together and add to the wet mixture.

Pour into a greased loaf pan and bake for about 1 hour or until a knife inserted in the middle comes out clean.

This classic Mediterranean dish is easy to make and is great when you're serving a large group of people.
Vary the recipe by substituting your favourite nut meats, or by adding a bit of chopped ginger or dried apricot.

Baklava

serves about 16

Preheat oven to 350°F

- *2 cups water*
- *1 cup sugar*
- *5 tablespoons honey*
- *$1/4$ cup lemon juice*
- *Splash of rose water (optional)*
- *1 teaspoon orange zest*
- *1 teaspoon cinnamon*
- *1 teaspoon nutmeg*
- *2 cups walnut pieces*
- *1 cup crushed almonds*
- *1 package phyllo pastry*
- *1 cup unsalted butter, melted*

Boil the water, sugar, honey and lemon juice together until it reaches a thick syrup-like consistency, about 10 minutes. Add a splash of rosewater and reserve at room temperature.

Mix the orange zest, cinnamon and nutmeg together with the nuts.

Lay a sheet of phyllo on a baking sheet and brush with melted butter. Place another sheet on top and brush with butter. Repeat four times. Spread one third of the nut mixture evenly over the sheets. Add four more layers of buttered phyllo. Add nut mixture and more phyllo, repeating until nut mixture is used up, finishing with a final single layer of buttered phyllo. Form cross hatches across the top with a knife.

Bake for 30 minutes. Lower the oven to 300°F and bake for another 30–45 minutes or until the pastry is golden brown. Pour the reserved syrup over the baklava and let cool.

This Baklava was made cutting phyllo dough into circles which were then buttered and stacked three high and baked until crisp.
To assemble we simply layered the phyllo with the nut mixture. Baklava is pictured here garnished with a riot of caramelized sugar.

If there's one thing I've learned about chai it's that everybody makes it a bit differently.
This recipe is one that my husband Ash and I have worked on for a while. Once you get the basics down it's fun to experiment.

Ash and Sarah's Chai Tea

serves 4

- 4 cups water
- 1 large cinnamon stick or 1/2 teaspoon ground cinnamon
- 1 1/2 teaspoons ground cardamom
- 1 teaspoon fennel seeds
- 2–3 whole cloves
- 1/8 teaspoon powdered ginger (optional)
- 1/8 teaspoon amchoor (mango powder) (optional)
- 4 regular tea bags
- 2–3 cups whole milk
- Sugar to taste

Mix the water and spices together and bring to a boil. Reduce to a simmer and add the tea bags. Allow to steep until desired strength is achieved. Add milk and bring to a simmer. Add sugar to taste, or serve unsweetened and allow each person to sweeten the tea to taste. This chai is excellent served with Writer's Block Cookies (recipe page 92).

This recipe comes from Vij's, our favourite restaurant in Vancouver.

Vij's Ginger-Lemon Drink

serves 4

- 1/4 lb fresh unpeeled ginger
- 1/2 cup plus 3 tablespoons fresh lemon juice
- 3 1/2 tablespoons sugar
- 3/4 teaspoon salt
- 4 cups sparkling water (or plain water) chilled

Finely grate the ginger. Using your hands, squeeze juice from ginger into a small bowl. Make sure there is no ginger pulp in the juice. Combine 4 teaspoons of ginger juice with the lemon juice, sugar and salt. Stir well and pour equal amounts into four glasses. Stir one cup of sparkling water into each glass.

Index

Admiration and thanks to the following:

My fantastic band: Ashwin Sood, Brian Minato, Sean Ashby, David Sinclair, Camille Henderson, and Vince Jones

My crew for all their hard work and dedication: Dan Fraser, Paul Runnals, Diane Johnston-Fraser, Dan Garnett, Joe Self, Al Robb, Dave Pallett, Gary Stokes, Graeme Nicol, Gavin Bakewell, Dean Warren, Jeff Marshall, Kevin McCloy, Isaac Kinakin, Tracey Ploss, Jennifer Bernard, Terry Mueller, Gary Radakovich, Gord Reddy, Dave Retson, Wally Cox, Albert Lovelace, Colette Van Loon, Steve Headley, JP Newton, Mikey Boivin, Dean Zurowski, Peter Grant, Rocky Sutherland, Deb Sutherland

Jaime Laurita for making touring such an enjoyable culinary experience
Kharen Hill for her wonderful pictures
Todd Merrel for his brilliant food styling
John Rummen for his great art direction
Crystal Heald for bringing all the pieces together and for her live photos
Nicola Piffaretti for his lovely design
and to Cathryn France for making this book possible

Additional thanks to:

Terry McBride, Michael Hurwitz, Matt Macdonald, Lori Hryhoruk, Jayne Craig, Eric Milner, Johnny Bellas, Vikram Vij, Alexandria Stuart, Sondra McLeod, Dorice McLachlan, Tracy Harvey, Cathy Barrett, Katharine Perak, Kathryn Hayashi, Neil K. Guy, Pat Coppard, Bob Mussell, Shaira Holman, and Al Robb for his on-the-road photos

Special thanks to Diana and Ray Towers for letting us turn their house upside down
Thanks and love to Ash for putting up with having our home taken over for this project
Thanks to Rex for taking Ash out for walks to keep him sane

Acknowledgements

And from Jaime

Thanks to:
My mother Annette Laurita for believing in me even when I was being unbelievable. I hope this book brings a smile to your beautiful face and a bit of the peace and comfort you so deserve. I love you with all my heart
My father Joseph and my ten brothers and sisters
My great, patient editor, Cathryn France
All the talented people at Madrigal Press and Nettwerk, especially John Rummen, Crystal Heald and Nicola Piffaretti
Kharen Hill and Todd Merrel "the proofs are in the pudding"
Rich Lane, Keli Bates, Diana Towers, Michael Hurwitz, John Traub and Debbie Sharpe for all their help

Additional thanks to Co-Co and Kim Van Loon, Albert Lovelace, and Tom Cassarro—my kitchen cronies and friends—"a great road team"

A huge thank you to all the roadies, crew, artists, and band members who have endlessly thanked and inspired me to "keep on cookin'" even when the heat was too hot to be in the kitchen

And of course, thanks to the wonderful Sarah McLachlan, whose overflowing generosity and exuberant love of my cuisine has enabled me to share my passion openly and honestly with you all. Her amazing voice is just the garnish to her poetic soul.
Thank you from the bottom of my heart...now let's cook!

Chef Jaime Laurita

Jaime has cooked everywhere from family
restaurants to top-notch professional
kitchens. He's a graduate of the Culinary
Institute of America, where he was awarded
a scholarship to the Italian Culinary
Institute for Foreigners. The scholarship
included an extensive tour of Italy, a
history of gastronomy, and of course food
and wine—lots of it!

Jaime studied in Italy for over a year,
training with some of that country's most
renowned chefs. He then travelled through
France where he learned the secrets of
many small bistros, as well as the haute
cuisine of some five star leaders.

Jaime brings all this experience and talent
together catering for many celebrities
and rock bands, including the Rolling Stones,
Placido Domingo, Barenaked Ladies,
The Tragically Hip, Phil Collins, and Prince.
This is his first cookbook.